# THE HAPPY READER

**BRING AN UMBRELLA**
Issue nº 8 — Autumn 2016

## PART 1

Bookish chancing, autumnal murmurs, and a tale of with KRISTIN SCOTT THOMAS.

| | |
|---|---|
| Risky | 5 |
| Snippets | 6 |
| The Interview: KRISTIN SCOTT THOMAS | 8 |
|     by Eva Wiseman — *A readerly assignation with an Anglo-Parisian luminary* | |
| Kristin's Paris reads | 31 |

## PART 2

Willa Cather's O PIONEERS! is Book of the Season, with basement memoirs, exotic barns, the philosophy of pageants and the psychology of pickles.

| | |
|---|---|
| Introduction: The plains are enormous | 35 |
|     by Seb Emina | |
| Communication: Hello there! | 36 |
|     by John Self — *If you're going to shout, make sure it counts* | |
| Comic: Neighboring fields | 37 |
|     by Dash Shaw — *Carl has news for Alexandra* | |
| Travel: Exciting, empty road | 39 |
|     by Clancy Martin — *Asking directions to a fictional town* | |
| Miss Nebraska | 44 |
|     by Yelena Moskovich — *Talents, pageants and the American experiment* | |
| Post-factual pioneer | 46 |
|     by Alexander Zaitchik — *Alex Jones's baffling monologues* | |
| Food: Preserverance | 48 |
|     by Bee Wilson — *Pickles are gifts from our past selves, but are they good gifts?* | |
| Encounter: Willa's wanders | 50 |
|     by Charlie Connelly — *You don't know me but I travelled a long way to meet you* | |
| A spotter's guide to the birds and barns of Nebraska | 52 |
| Memory: Do not enter | 56 |
|     by Amanda Fortini — *Once upon a summer in a Kansas suburb* | |
| Letters | 61 |
| The next book | 62 |

The quilt that inspired this pattern was stitched by the Nebraska State Quilt Guild. It is held in Lincoln, Nebraska, at the International Quilt Study Center & Museum.

THE HAPPY READER

British photographer DAVID HURN noticed, and captured, this mysterious bookshop window in the city of Simrishamn, Sweden.

THE HAPPY READER

# RISKY

What book should I read next? It's a question that pretends to be more casual than it is. Sometimes the answer will be carefully considered. Do I seek out that popular title I keep seeing everywhere, the one that is ostensibly about working as an office temp in Iceland but is really an uplifting memoir about the human condition? Or is it more a case of: I'll just nonchalantly pick up a yellowed paperback in this bed and breakfast and hope it reveals itself to be an accomplished, unfairly-forgotten literary thriller? It would seem the former is the more failsafe method on the basis that, as with choosing a bank account or booking a flight, it is prudent to consider one's options. But in the case of books, it's complicated by a simple but often overlooked fact: premeditation affects our enjoyment. Expectations change everything.

Consider the way that a song we would never dream of seeking out will sound wonderful when it just happens to be what's emanating from the radio in the back of a cab: a lack of choice can be intoxicating, and from time to time, it is fun to radioify our reading. Or to brazenly switch analogies, to embark on what book critic Robert McCrum has called 'the literary equivalent of hitchhiking'. He was specifically writing about his habit of limiting holiday reading to whatever he comes across during a trip, a practice which, 'provides many of the same pleasures as taking to the open road.' A recently-published essay collection, *Browse: The World in Bookshops*, contains many odes to the joy of chance reading. In her contribution, Ali Smith hails the 'unexpected repositories' that show up in the donations pile at the charity bookshop where she volunteers — from *Hunter's Guide to Grasses, Clovers and Weeds* to D.H. Lawrence's *Birds, Beasts and Flowers*. Mark Forsyth, quoted in the introduction, argues that, as far as books are concerned, 'the best things are the things you never knew you wanted until you got them.'

It'd be ridiculous to say that we should rule out deciding what book to read next, or that the act of choosing ruins everything. But it's also true that childhood, the time most of us remember as containing the best reading experiences of our lives, was a time when almost every book was picked up at random. The sheer innocent pleasure of just reading whatever's to hand is something we tend to sideline as we get older, more rational, more time-conscious. We neglect it to our detriment. Of course, we encourage you to hunt down every issue of *The Happy Reader* with a cult-like fervour, but if you did just come across this issue, and have no idea what it is, then please, please, read on.

THE HAPPY READER
Bookish Quarterly
Issue nº 8 — Autumn 2016

The Happy Reader is a collaboration between Penguin Books and Fantastic Man

EDITOR-IN-CHIEF
Seb Emina

EDITORIAL DIRECTORS
Jop van Bennekom
Gert Jonkers

MANAGING EDITOR
Cecilia Stein

DESIGN
Tom Etherington

DESIGN CONCEPT
Jop van Bennekom
Helios Capdevila

PRODUCTION
Charlotte Veaney

PUBLISHER
Stefan McGrath

MARKETING DIRECTOR
Nicola Hill

BRAND MANAGER
Sam Voulters

PICTURE RESEARCH
Samantha Johnson

CONTRIBUTORS
Charlie Connelly, Amanda Fortini, Eliot Haworth, David Hurn, Clancy Martin, Yelena Moskovich, Katja Rahlwes, Megan Wray Schertler, John Self, Dash Shaw, Bee Wilson, Eva Wiseman, Alexander Zaitchik.

THANK YOU
Magnus Åkesson, Alice Cavanagh, Baxter, Lauren Elkin, Annabelle Fernandez, Mike Fitzgerald, Jordan Kelly, Christian Lorentzen, Penny Martin, Sabine Mirlesse, Rebecca Morris, Rosa Rankin-Gee, Megan Roberts, Sarah Polak, Sylvia Whitman.

Penguin Books
80 Strand
London WC2R 0RL

info@thehappyreader.com
www.thehappyreader.com

Image: © David Hurn / Magnum Photos

5

THE HAPPY READER

# SNIPPETS

Curious happenings and alluring occasions from the world of printed sentences.

HUH — When logging onto Amazon, a Londoner was irked to find a hacker had used her account to purchase no less than twenty-seven books. A particularly puzzling element of the crime, from a moral point of view, was that every one of the titles that the cyber-crook had purchased was on the subject of 'being a good Christian'.

\*

EQUESTRIAN — The bookselling world was sent into a frenzy by the triumph of 58-year-old equestrian Nick Skelton at the Rio Olympics. When Skelton won top honours in individual showjumping, becoming Britain's oldest gold medalist since 1908, his out-of-print autobiography *Only Falls and Horses* became the most sought-after title on bookselling website AbeBooks. Scarce copies of the book, which was published in 2001 by now-defunct publisher Greenwater, have rocketed in value, currently fetching around £500 each.

\*

WELL READ — How long would it take to read all the books in the world? Well, in 2010, Google estimated the total number of objects created by humanity that qualify as 'books' to be 129,864,880, an impossible-to-verify figure calculated by analysing a huge variety of sources such as libraries and union catalogues. Recently a journalist named Roma Panganiban took an educated guess at the updated, mid-2016 total, and came up with the number 134,021,533, meaning that, not including those released in the latter half of this year and assuming the reader in question is able to sustain an impressive rate of three books per week, it would take 859,112 years to read all the books in the world.

Illustration: Yann Le Bec

# SNIPPETS

BOUND — The book collection of Coco Chanel is currently on display at Ca' Pesaro Gallery in Venice. The fashion designer, an enthusiastic bibliophile whose favourite authors included Homer, Michel de Montaigne and Madame de Sévigné, commissioned a custom range of beautiful art deco covers from the celebrated bookbinder Germaine Schroeder. The exhibition, entitled *The Woman Who Reads*, runs until 8 January 2017.

*

URN — The ashes of Truman Capote, the American author of *Breakfast at Tiffany's* and *In Cold Blood*, have been bought at auction in Los Angeles for $43,750. Having previously been the property of Capote's friend Joanne Carson, who died last year the remains were acquired after a bidding battle, by an anonymous collector.

*

VIOLENT — J. K. Rowling listened to the Violent Femmes' eponymous album for the first time, and hated it. The Harry Potter creator was taking part in the excellent 'Ruth and Martin's Album Club', in which notable figures listen to classic records that have somehow passed them by then report back via Ruth and Martin's website. Her low opinion of 1983's *Violent Femmes* was, she said, due to lead singer Gordon Gano's voice, describing it as 'like a bee in a plastic cup'. However, Rowling had a significant change of heart on her second airing ('This is weird. The vocalist is actually, um... good') and by the third was a raging fan, awarding multimillion-selling album the solid-to-fantastic mark of 8.5/10.

*

UNION — As tends to be the way with these now-ubiquitous swap-spots, the free library at Arsenal underground station in London is both a convenient place to find a book and a handy place to get rid of one. Following the UK's vote to leave the European Union, it has received an exasperated glut of titles on the subject of EU law.

*

ALWAYS BACK UP — A New Orleans man dashed into a burning building to save his only copies of two completed novels. Having hurried home from work after his fiancée called to inform him their house was on fire, Gideon Hodge, thirty-five, realised the laptop on which the manuscripts were saved was still inside. Ignoring the shouts of firefighters he bolted through the smoke and somehow retrieved the computer from beneath the table where it had fortunately been sheltered from the hose-water. 'Anybody that's ever created art, there's no replacing that,' he told the *New Orleans Advocate*. But are the novels as daring as their author?

*

PARADISE — The house in which F. Scott Fitzgerald lived while completing his debut novel *This Side of Paradise* has been put on sale. Situated on the leafy, sought-after Summit Ave in St Paul, Minnesota, the 3,500-square-foot property has an asking price of $625,000. Buyers will enjoy a stream of Fitzgerald fans, who turn up daily to gaze at the building in which the *Great Gatsby* author lived with his parents during his early twenties.

Uttering the name 'Kristin Scott Thomas' will often produce a concise but telling response: 'I love her!!!' The English actress's mighty cultural status comes as much from her singular off-screen personality as it does from her celebrated roles in movies such as *The English Patient* and *Four Weddings and a Funeral* and stage productions including *The Seagull* and *Electra*. A resident of Paris since she was a teenager, Scott Thomas is a frequent patron of the famed, labyrinthine bookshops that contribute so much to the city's headily erudite atmosphere. Across two in-depth meetings, she tells *The Happy Reader* how it is to live, and work, in a perpetual whirl of well-chosen words.

# KRISTIN SCOTT THOMAS

In conversation with
EVA WISEMAN

Portraits by
KATJA RAHLWES

---

DAME KRISTIN
SCOTT THOMAS
(24-05-60)

Born in: Redruth, Cornwall. Lives in: Paris, France. Film debut: *Under the Cherry Moon* (1986, dir: Prince). Awards include: a BAFTA for Best Supporting Actress (for *Four Weddings and a Funeral*) and an Olivier Award for Best Actress (for *The Seagull*). Films include: *Bitter Moon* (1992), *The English Patient* (1996), *Gosford Park* (2001). Height: 1.68m. Children: 3. Siblings: 5. Rank in French Legion of Honour system: *officier*. Middle name: Ann.

## LONDON

I meet Kristin Scott Thomas in a cafe on a hot, rom-com sort of afternoon. She is fifty-six and cardigan-ed, and a great beauty of the kind found in religious art. I say a cafe — it's the Mount Street Deli in Mayfair, a small wood-panelled coffee shop seen only in Hollywood films about London. We'll meet twice — once in London, and once in Paris — she lives between the two. In Mayfair she appears the quintessential English woman, almost tweedy; when In France, the ultimate Parisian. It's a combination, perhaps, of ease, and good acting.

Scott Thomas was born in Cornwall. When she was five, her father died in a flying accident. Her mother remarried, to another pilot; six years later, he too died flying. At nineteen, told by her teacher she'd never be an actress because she had 'no talent and was useless', she moved to France to become an au pair. In Paris, encouraged by her boss, she studied drama; her first job was opposite Prince, in his 1986 directorial debut *Under the Cherry Moon*. She's worked steadily since, winning a BAFTA for *Four Weddings and a Funeral*, and an Oscar nomination for *The English Patient*. Her second career (third, if you count au pairing) was in French cinema, with another handful of award nominations. And then, after having her third child, she announced she'd given up film. Done. She was walking the dog early one morning, and stopped without knowing why. She looked down at the pavement, and saw a piece of blue tape, of the sort used to mark out places on movie sets, and realised her body had instinctively told her not to cross the line. So she stopped, not just in the street, but in the industry. Her next career was on the stage. She played Electra, she played the Queen. She became a Dame. It's her damehood, she tells me, with theatrical flourish, that allows her to change her mind.

KRISTIN: My friend, who runs the Shakespeare and Company bookshop, showed me *The Happy Reader* — that's why I'm here. I came across this bookshop years and years ago when I first moved to Paris. It was dark and dingy and a bit mysterious and kind of scary.

EVA: Why scary?

K: Well, because it was so intimidating. There was a very ancient man who ran it who could either be completely beastly or completely wonderful, depending on whether he approved of what you were looking at. I was nineteen and would go, sort of longing for somebody to say, 'Come in, I'll introduce you.' And then about five years ago I was working with Ethan Hawke and Pawel Pawlikowski and getting quite irritated by them going on and on about how marvellous this woman 'Sylvia' was. Turns out she is the daughter of the scary old man and she runs the shop — she's super-young, super-enthusiastic, with brilliant ideas. I've seen some great things there. Martin Amis and Will Self doing a kind of double act, Lydia Davis, Don DeLillo...

E: Do you buy your books there as well?

K: Mostly I buy my English books there. My French books I buy in this fantastic place just opposite me, where you always have to queue for ten minutes behind old people buying religious books. But as you know, bookshops are closing — every time you blink one closes. I love bookshops, but sometimes I become overwhelmed and buy the thing they're pushing and get home and open it and it's AWFUL.

E: Do you have to finish books?

K: No. I don't stay until the end of plays either. It's a bit like therapy, you know, this is my time, I've paid for it. I've got from 7.30pm to 9.30pm and if I don't like it I will leave.

E: I once saw a play on a first date. And we left, walking along the South Bank really moved by it, and it was kind of magical... But then the next day I got a call from this guy saying he'd happened to meet the director of the play at a party. It turned out we'd left in the middle.

K: Oh God — did you go back?

E: He did. He said it all tied up so neatly that the story was ruined.

K: Oh, how brilliant. Did you see the guy again?

E: No.

K: No! I love that story. I change the ends of books as well. Do you remember the end of *Cold Mountain*? They're all sitting around the fire? Well, I read the thing imagining that his wife was waiting back home and then it all worked out in the end. When of course they're all dead. Somebody said to me, 'Oh God, I've just finished it, bit of a downer at the end,' and I said, 'No it's not, it's wonderful!' I'd completely, you know, made it mine.

E: Do you write?

K: No, I just have no self-discipline. I've got loads of ideas, but I've tried everything, longhand, computers, and I'll get maybe 400 words done and then I'll go, 'Just need to check my messages...'

1. SOMETIMES LESS
—
The American author Lydia Davis, whose stories are often just a few sentences or even a single sentence long, was given a lifetime achievement award by *The Paris Review* this year. To celebrate they collaborated with the cosmetics brand Aesop to reprint one of her oldest stories, 'Spring Spleen', on the side of a bottle of mouthwash. The story is exactly 20 words long.

E: Lydia Davis manages to tell a story in 100 words.

K: And sometimes less. I love that. I love the concentration of it. And there's a sort of distance, a space in all of them, in spite of having only two or three lines. Within those lines there's an entire world.

E: Do you read plays?

K: I hate reading plays. When you have to do all the voices yourself... ugh. I prefer novels. I'm reading *The Europeans* again, Henry James. It's great, and it's old! I love second-hand books. There's something very reassuring about them because they've been used already.

E: It's proven to work.

K: There was a book, it's a bestseller at the moment, and to begin with I thought, oh God, this is just nonsense, and then I can't say what it is because —

E: Off the record.

K: Off the record, do you promise?

E: Yeah.

K: It's called [REDACTED].

E: Oh, I thought it was dire too.

K: Oh, thank God for that. I get very cross about too many words, I do, I get very cross about it, which is why I like Lydia Davis because it's so spare. I also like funny books. Anything from Alan Bennett to Bridget Jones. The books that have made me laugh the most recently are Teddy St Aubyn's.

E: Is he a friend of yours?

K: He's become a friend of mine because I read his novels, then went to the bookshop and met him.

E: Are you a bit of an author groupie?

K: As far as he was concerned, yes. There's something completely fascinating about somebody who can make up whole worlds in their heads. I've always got about four books on the go because I give up so easily. Somebody gave me a book the other day, and the first line was something like, 'Until his wife declared that she was a vegetarian he thought she was unremarkable in every way' [*The Vegetarian*, by Han Kang], which I thought was just a brilliant first line. And it's the first that gets you, isn't it?

E: Do you ever read something and then think, I must adapt this?

K: Yes, but it's such a hard thing to do. I've been adapting an Elizabeth Jane Howard novel, *The Sea Change*, for ages. I first read it when I was seventeen and at last we got it right with Rebecca Lenkiewicz, the writer of the film *Ida*. She's written a beautiful, loose adaptation. We'd been trying to get it off the ground for ages, and until I'm actually in front of the camera doing it, I won't believe it's ever going to happen. But Elizabeth Jane Howard is such a brilliant observer of character, of people being careful in their behaviour.

E: What's the story?

K: Well, our film is the story of a couple. He's a writer, she's a sort of facilitator, and it's to do with infidelities and loss and mourning and how to climb back out of misery. It should make you feel good when you leave the cinema, but it's quite dark to begin with and it gets happier and happier as it goes on. It's a love story.

E: How does the collaboration work with you and Rebecca?

K: Well, we've already had three or four versions from other people and they were never really getting it. And then we said to her, 'Forget about the book, forget about everything else, just take it away and write what you want to write with the story in your head,' which is what she did. So it's got away from the terror of adapting such a book from such a… I'm not going to say restrained, but 'reined in' period piece. She wrote it in 1959, so people don't behave like this any more, but their feelings are the same. It's just the way we behave about them that changes. Whether you decide to hide it or declare it. We let her get on with it, and then we sit down and I say something like, 'I'd like a bit more of that there,' then I go through and check her spelling. It's how I deal with control.

E: You change the font size?

K: Basically. There are some things I can't stand in screenwriting. I don't like it when writers put ums and ahs and dot, dot, dots. I like a line to be clean so that an actor can then do what he wants with it. There are various other things — there's the very modern way of speaking I don't like.

E: Do you mean like, a 'like'?

K: Yes. The other thing is 'she is sat', that's the thing that I can't stand. She is sitting! The words that really annoy me are all words about acquisition… OK, a perfect example. So and so says he wants to 'gift' you something. What does that exactly mean? The gifting becomes a part of the exchange. If they wanted to give it to me then that's clear, all done. But, gifting…

2. THE SEA CHANGE

Elizabeth Jane Howard's 1959 novel of a marriage in crisis is not to be confused with the 2013 book of the same name by Joanna Rossiter that documents a woman's recollections in the debris of a Tsunami. Nor is it to be confused with a raft of similarly named titles including the emotional thriller by Karen White about a recently married woman who moves to a remote Georgian island, the historical crime novel set in 18th century London by Robert Goddard and the aquatic fantasy romance by Aimee Friedman.

3. 1959

A big year for spacecraft, including:
— The launch of 'Corona' (USA), the first operational spy satellite.
— The launch of 'Luna 1' (Soviet Union, pictured), the first spacecraft to escape Earth's gravitational influence.
— The launch of 'Jupiter AM-18' (USA), a missile containing squirrel monkeys Able and Baker, the first living beings to successfully return from space to Earth.

THE HAPPY READER

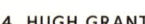

4. HUGH GRANT
—
There exists an adult colouring book entitled *The Life and Times of Hugh Grant* featuring many of the actor's most famous moments, including the infamous mid-90s mugshot.

5. YOU BECOME A NUMBER
—
In the popular parlour game *Six Degrees of Kevin Bacon*, Kristin Scott Thomas has a Bacon Number of two, meaning she is two degrees of separation from American actor Kevin Bacon. The route: Scott Thomas appeared in 1998's *The Revengers' Comedies* with Helena Bonham Carter; Bonham Carter appeared in 2001's *Novocaine* with Kevin Bacon.

E: You're complicit?

K: You're complicit in it, there's an expectation of an exchange. There's something to your advantage if you 'gift' somebody something, whereas if you give it, it's just a present. Am I completely nuts?

E: Not completely.

K: I just get more upset about that than the fact that no one's actually agreed to do the film with me.

E: Have you fancied directing for a while?

K: Yes, I get so frustrated. I'm sure it will be incredibly difficult because you have to keep eight different thoughts in your head at once, which is not my particular forte, but I think if you get a really good group of people around you it can be done.

E: Surely you're in a perfect position to say, 'This is what I want and this is the film that I want to make'?

K: That doesn't mean to say it's ever going to happen. First of all we've got to find a man, you can't do anything without a man.

E: Never.

K: Distributors give you a list of about four people, including Leonardo DiCaprio and Hugh Grant, who are wildly inappropriate. It's the same for me. I can't get hired, even though I'm the right person for the job, because I'm not famous enough or, you know, I'm not hot enough. That's what they call bankability, isn't it?

E: God, is there a chart?

K: Oh, you're going to love this. OK, I went up for a job not very long ago that I really wanted, and I got a call from my American agent who said, 'I'm sorry, but they've just run the numbers and it's not going to work.' Literally, you become a number. The numbers that they run are how many films you've made, how many people have seen them, how much profit each made. If you're at the top of the list you're all right, and if you've been working for thirty years and your numbers are below average, well.

E: How do you deal with that?

K: I don't really deal with it, I just put one foot in front of the other rather blindly and plod on. I had a bit of a crisis about three years ago and said I will not make any more films, that's it, over. And I really devoted myself to theatre and I loved working onstage, the whole engagement of it, but it is an absolute killer. And because the kind of things that I'm interested in are pretty intense usually, I can't

14

really do two things back to back. If you work in the theatre a lot, then afterwards when you go and do a film you're always much better because everything's warmed up and your brain works quicker. You get a bit stagnant when you're working on films. Because you're sitting there waiting to go, with one scene in your head, no air going through.

E: You said you were finished with films.

K: But I'm a Dame and I'm allowed to change my mind. So, I'm now going to do a film with a brilliant director called Sally Potter. It's an experiment really, that's the sort thing that interests me. Rather than, you know, put on a wig, stand on a mark and look upset, angry, icy, pitying, withering, whatever, you know. Snore, can't be bothered. It suddenly dawned on me that I was spending more time pretending I was someone else in a year than I was actually being me.

E: What does that do to you?

K: It's not right. You just stop, you know. I've got fewer children at home now, so I don't have the anxiety of bringing them up. One sixteen-year-old son at home, one son lurking on the threshold because he's being an actor and he's broke, and then my daughter, who's a writer, she works for *The New York Times*. She's meeting me here soon actually, we've got to go and look at wedding paraphernalia.

E: Are you excited about the wedding?

K: Yeah, I'm just really happy for her. And it's fun doing something when you're not the centre of attention. I'm sure I'll manage it.

E: Is there a book that taught you how to be you?

K: The book that made me understand how complicated it was to be a grown-up actually was this book that I'm trying to adapt. When I was young I identified with the young girl, and now that I'm older I identify with the middle-aged woman. And I used to love Jane Austen, I identified with that world of dignified poverty, trying desperately to hang on to the idea that things were OK.

E: Was that your life?

K: To a certain degree. In the country, everybody always had more money than we did, and I was trying to cling on to an idea of belonging somewhere, which is difficult because my father died when I was very little. It really does make you who you are. If my father had lived, I might not have gone to France, I might not have been an actress… I had quite a dramatic series of events that I think made me crave drama because drama was something I knew and could relate to and felt alive with. I'm very easily moved, I'm a terrible weeper.

6. WEDDING PARAPHERNALIA
—
An interesting turn of phrase because, as it happens, the word 'paraphernalia' is etymologically attached to weddings, based as it is on the Greek *parpherna*, meaning 'property apart from a dowry'. In its original fifteenth-century usage, this meant it referred to items that remained in a woman's ownership after marriage. (Today, of course, it means simply 'stuff'.)

E: Have you always been?

K: Yeah, and people always think I'm incredibly tough and not sentimental, but I am easily moved.

E: Why do people think you're tough?

K: Well, take for example the recent bad news that Prince died, right? Now, I had a relationship with him — he was the first person to pay me to be in a film and we kept in touch over all these years — and when he died I was sort of stuck with this feeling of... emptiness. Everyone is ringing me up saying, 'Oh my God, isn't it awful, can you believe it?' I couldn't relate to it at all in a personal way. I wasn't able to express the other connection. Not the woman who loved his songs and went to his concerts and sang along, not that woman, but the other woman, the woman who remembers... And so I automatically switch to try and help the person who is obviously upset. When you're the oldest, you have to deal with everybody else's sadness first and then you'll deal with your own.

E: So will that come, that sadness, when you have a moment alone?

K: I have had a little bit of a weep, I suppose, but there's nowhere really to put the grief, apart from doing my own little Prince evening at home with a couple of candles. It'd be nice to be involved in a ritual of some description. I've been to some really good funerals recently.

E: What makes a good one?

K: A friend of mine died a few months ago and it was the saddest thing in the world, but it was so great to feel the intense energy. How extraordinary, how beautiful it was to be able to express that. The thing that I get upset about in funerals is when people stand up to give their eulogy and it's all about them. How did we get on to funerals? It's a bit miserable. Oh, that thing of dealing with everybody else before you deal with your own stuff.

E: You're talking about a lot of things there, you're talking about being older and you're talking about being maternal.

K: About being responsible. A lot of people I've worked with have died, actually. Anyway, moving on. No, adapting novels is really hard — I mean, when we worked with Anthony Minghella and Michael Ondaatje, it was a marriage made in heaven, the film became a kind of sibling to the book, it ran along parallel. Such a wonderful feeling, because you don't feel any sense of betrayal. When it works it's great. Now a lot of books seem to be written with film rights in mind.

E: How do you feel about that?

K: I just wish there were more original screenplay writers. I love novels, I love the fact that you can just dive in and you've got a kind of ready-made rendezvous. I'm not very good at sleeping so I read at night. I used to read all the time, but that's quite dangerous when you're acting. I remember doing a film when I was in the throes of my passion for Jean Rhys, and one day the director said, 'Kristin, you've got to stop reading Jean Rhys, put it away.'

E: They could tell the difference?

K: Exactly, I was so miserable. I'm quite porous to sort of imagery like that, I do take it on board. Are you a Jonathan Franzen fan? When I get to the end of his books I start again. Sometimes it's unbearable that you're out of a book, you've been abandoned. That's what I felt like when I read *The Goldfinch*. I just couldn't bear not being with those people any more. Do you live in London?

E: Yes.

K: I'm a resident of England at the moment too. I can't stand all this privatisation of space. The thing that really disgusts me is the thirty-pound fee to go up to the top of the Shard.

E: Is it easy, living in two places?

K: No, it's bloody hard.

E: Where do you keep your books?

K: I'm just literally spilt down the middle, it's quite hard. Feel sorry for me! Hang on, I'll show you what the view is from my window in Paris.

E: Are you on Instagram?

K: Yeah. Love it. Look.

E: That's from your window?

K: Yeah, that's what I see from my bed.

E: What's the opposite of feeling sorry for you?

K: Jealous, covetous, envious?

E: Shall we finish there?

K: OK.

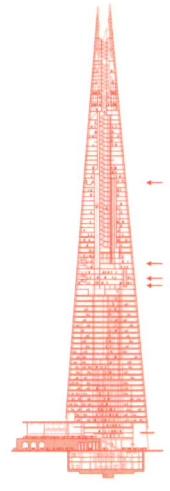

7. THE SHARD

The 'on the day' price to gain access to the top-floor viewing platform of this 72-storey building in Southwark, London, is a breathtaking £30.95. This figure or less might also purchase refreshments in any of the restaurants or bars on the 31st, 32nd, 35th and 52nd floors, all of which have windows.

Of the estimated 21,000 British citizens living in Paris, Scott Thomas may well be the most famous. Hair: Sebastien Richard. Makeup: Lisa Legrand.

# KRISTIN SCOTT THOMAS

## PARIS

Before I met Kristin Scott Thomas, I'd been warned that she was difficult. Icy. In my experience, though, words like this, like 'bossy', or 'quirky', are usually codes to talk about women that don't act the way you want them to. She confirmed that — she was professional, generous, dry. The day after we met she found my email address online and sent me a message, signed 'KST'.

She arrives a minute after me, slipping into a booth in the cafe opposite a wedding-dress shop, and shrugging off an oversized grey coat with a grin. She appears more relaxed in Paris. She shakes my hand.

E: I'm reading your book.
K: Which one? *The Vegetarian*?

E: No, the...
K: *The Europeans*?

E: No.
K: Joseph Roth.

E: No.
K: Oh, God. I've read more than three?

E: *The Sea Change*.
K: Oh, you found it!

E: The weird thing is, I find I read it in your voice.
K: Ha. We're trying to get the characters as near to the novel as possible, especially the girl, because I love that girl. But of course finding a girl like that nowadays is virtually impossible.

E: Why?
K: Because I think girls nowadays are far less idealistic in the human condition. I think they're much more cynical. Because of 'social meeja'.

E: Is that your real accent coming through there?
K: Yeah! Seriously though, the way you deal with your feelings and how you're expected to behave, it's different because of social

media. It's all because of this story about image. I had a great long lecture about that on Sunday from my eldest son, the philosopher.

E: What did he say?

K: Something really clever. It just goes, whoosh, straight over my head. He's trying to get off the social media. I think there is a section of people who are the equivalent of what hippies were when I was growing up, the people who are trying to unhook from all that stuff about what you look like — you know, who are you? I am this person here, right now, sitting here, not some kind of... cipher.

E: I agree, but I'm wary of people who try to deny it entirely and completely ignore it. Because it's not another place; it's where we live now.

K: Absolutely. And that's what he was sort of worrying about, the fact that the only alternative seems to be going into this kind of strange Utopic environment, which he is not willing to do. He doesn't want to cut off from everybody; he just wants to be able to communicate on his own terms.

E: We should be able to learn to navigate it without losing our soul.

K: It's things like reading, for example, which you used to do to relax. I found this on Sunday. I thought, 'Great, I'm going to be able to settle down with my book and I'll be happy.' But all the time the computer was saying to me, 'I've got really interesting things in here...' So I spent an hour desperately shopping for wall clocks. I find it very invasive actually, because you don't take time to DO things any more.

E: I don't think it's just about the phone or the computer; I think it's about our minds.

K: Yeah, but it's the way we adapt to it. Of course it's about our minds. It's about the way that relaxing is no longer about taking out your novel and plunging into the world of God knows what. It starts with, 'Ooh, and what does this word mean?' And then you look it up, and you can just go on... I completely understand why Jonathan Franzen glued up his USB plugs.

E: His novel *Freedom* has the same name as the computer program that blocks your internet.

K: Oh, that's good.

E: I read a little bit about *The Sea Change*. In Elizabeth Jane Howard's obituary it mentioned that every day she wrote precisely 300 words.

8. CLOCKS

'Stop all the clocks,' goes the opening to W. H. Auden's 'Funeral Blues', the devastating poem recited during the 'funeral' section of *Four Weddings and a Funeral*. Last year, sales of wall clocks in the UK alone were worth £4.65m, and stopping them all would take, alas, almost forever.

**9. ESKIMO WORD**

This may be 'itsuarok', often translated as 'the frustration and uncertainty of waiting for someone to show up'. A handy untranslatable word for avid readers is 'tsundoku', a Japanese term meaning 'the act of buying a book and leaving it unread, typically next to a pile of other unread books'.

**10. THIRTY-FIVE**

Those currently experiencing what it is to be thirty-five include Tom Hiddleston, Amy Schumer, Justin Timberlake and Serena Williams.

K: Did she! She was the most extraordinary woman, very striking and very strong. A lot of her books have been adapted for screen. Those Cazalet stories, those are all hers. But this is a bit different because it gets out of the Englishness somehow. That's one of the themes of the story, isn't it? How to be who you are when you're longing for someone else. I remember when they did the adaptation of *The English Patient* as well, that seemed to be totally impossible to do, because there are two parallel stories. But the end result is a miracle. To turn a novel like that into something that works on screen requires such a lot of self-control and I would say lack of *orgueil*, of... pride?

E: Does that happen often, where you lose an English word?

K: Yeah. Less and less, because I speak more English now. I must have been insufferable twenty years ago. I don't know how anyone put up with me. But there are some words that are just better in French and some that are better in English. Somebody recently published a list of words that were untranslatable in certain languages. Most of them had lots of syllables and described very complicated sentiments. Like, there's an Eskimo word for the feeling that you get when you're waiting for someone that you haven't seen for a long time to appear.

E: Aren't we magical?
K: We are.

E: Reading *The Sea Change*, I was thinking about the debate around female characters being likeable.
K: Well, these ones certainly aren't.

E: And having read all those interviews with you and how people have described you in the past as icy...

K: Oh, I hate it. I found a shoebox full of those tiny little mini-cassettes. There was twenty years of film there. I put it all on DVD and spent the weekend with my son watching their childhood. It's amazed me both how much we've changed and how little we've changed, in that the body language is exactly the same. It's absolutely extraordinary how someone who is eight still has the same mannerisms and grumpiness about certain things at twenty-eight. It's amazing. And we started that when I was thirty-five. To see how I've changed, and how... hard I seemed to be before. I thought, 'Wow. No wonder they thought I was icy.'

E: Why were you hard?
K: It's like a kind of... wariness, I guess. A sort of, 'Don't attack me, because if you do I'll attack you.' A defensive thing.

E: Was it related to fame?

K: It's about not knowing the truth. It's about that wariness of, 'Are you lying?' Which of course comes a lot with fame. You get a lot of lies when you're famous. 'Oh, you're so beautiful. You're so talented.' You're frightened of taking it seriously, because God knows what would happen to you then.

E: Do you feel vulnerable, in your work?

K: No, because it's not really me. You said you were reading that book in my voice. That's my job, and how amazing, right? My first thing was Brenda Last in Evelyn Waugh. What a gift, to be able to walk into that world and come out of it unscathed, but to express those fears or that longing.

E: So, your work comes from wanting to go deeper into stories?

K: I think so, yeah. I've always been fascinated by people who can actually write stories. I've been tempted to try... Luckily for you...

E: Oh, for a second I thought you were bringing out a manuscript.

K: Ha! People have asked me to write things, but I'm just not any good at it.

E: Why do you think that?

K: I'm very good at email, but I've got no self-discipline.

E: Three hundred words a day.

K: But then I get to the bottom of my paragraph and I'd want to start over completely — basically going off on tangents all the time. Great for psychoanalysis; terrible for writing. Which is why I'm always drawn to performance rather than pure creativity, because there are such strict tracks to stick on. But the greatest thrill is actually having your face on the cover of a book. It's pathetic, isn't it? Miss Literary Adaptation.

E: But then it's as if you've written it.

K: I'm having terrible problems with that word, 'adaptation', recently, because in French I keep saying 'adaptation' and in English I say 'adaption'. Once I said, 'I've got a terrible gangster in my throat,' meaning I had a frog in my throat. *Un crapaud* is very similar to *crapule*. So *crapaud* is a frog and *crapule* is a gangster. Actually it's more like a thug. 'I've got a terrible thug in my throat.'

E: At the same time you seem to be the proper English lady and the ultimate French madame. Is that cultivated?

K: No, not at all. I caught a glimpse of myself in the shop window today and I literally thought, 'What's that?'

E: Why?

K: Did you ever see the Belgian photographers who went round the world photographing people from various social groups? Hilarious. Thanks to globalisation of the clothing market, every town has a version of the same thing. We all belong to dressing tribes. I don't think fashion is important, but clothes are. They tell you an awful lot.

E: So when you saw yourself in the shop window, what did you see?

K: What did I think? 'Who is that lady from Sherborne in Dorset?' When I took my son to school in England and he was very little, I thought, 'Oh God, I'm going to stick out like a sore thumb.' Anyway, I turned up — I'm exactly the same as every other middle-class mother taking her child to that school. Long blond hair, padded black coat, big pair of boots, huge handbags. We're all the same. So boring.

E: Do you ever read self-help books?

K: I have tried. I've been advised to by various friends.

E: Good friends.

K: That's why everybody loves those Kindles, because they can read whatever they like and no one will know. The first section of *The Vegetarian* is about a man whose wife stops eating meat and then goes completely doolally. The rest, I'm not telling you. No offence. This really is exhausting that you can't offend anybody any more. Don't you think?

E: Yeah. I think we should all have the right to offend and be offended.

K: Well, that's the whole point of life, isn't it?

E: Do you offend?

K: Oh, frequently. I get into trouble.

E: What was the last one?

K: No, we're not going to talk about this. I've been told never to mention it again.

E: Give me a clue.

K: *Daily Mail.* OK. You might have seen my face in various chemists going, 'I love it when people ask my age,' which of course is a massive lie. But the product is wonderful, so I was quite happy to lie for them. I was asked by a beauty magazine, 'What's the difference

11. SELF HELP BOOKS
—
With over 130 million copies sold, the most popular self help book ever is *Chicken Soup for the Soul*, in which Jack Canfield and Mark Victor Hansen collect a series of 'true testimonies of goodness'. Such has been the success of the original and its many follow-ups that the two have expanded their business into areas such as TV shows, pet food — and actual chicken soup.

between French and English women's ideals of beauty?' So then I trotted out a whole load of ridiculous generalisations about French women never eating anything, never brushing their hair, never getting dressed up in the evenings. My contrast to that was English women drink till they fall over, dye themselves orange and wear mini-skirts at fifty-three. Of course, that — 'Dame Kristin says British women are vulgar' and all the rest of it — went on for a whole week. The *Spectator*, the *Guardian*. I thought the fact that the *Daily Mail* put it on their front page was in itself hilarious. But then the rumpus it caused, people saying I was a snob, was...

E: Not?

K: You can't respond to the *Daily Mail*. It upsets the balance of your life; it upsets the balance of your children's lives, of your parents' lives. My mother freaks out. 'Darling, they're not being very kind about you in the *Daily Mail*.' Oh really, Mother?

E: Does it affect your work?

K: Well, it probably does affect my ability to work, but it doesn't affect how I work, just the possibility of work. I got a big shock once. I was doing a film, and the director told me the sexy young actress playing opposite me had been switched for a new one. 'Was she better than the other?' I asked. They said no, not really, but she had a very famous boyfriend and loads of Twitter followers. Wrong answer. Don't tell actors that.

E: In London you mentioned your 'crisis', when you decided not to make films any more. Was that experience related?

K: After a while all these things kind of mount up and you think, 'Oh, it's enough.' I just read a brilliant screenplay that I'm furious I can't do. It happens so rarely. The novel industry, if you like, has changed so much over the past twenty years.

E: How?

K: Novelists don't get paid anything any more. In the old days you used to get risks taken — I did one film where the book itself wasn't finished when the rights were bought. That's extraordinary, isn't it?

E: When you're not working, what do your days consist of?

K: Well, I've always got things to do, like looking after this project, *The Sea Change*. You're always backing up other projects. It's very rare that you're not being solicited in some way. The thing about my job is it's a lot of preparation. At the moment I'm learning the lines for my next thing. Then there's also living. Living itself gets quite busy.

E: There's a bit in the book about that — Lillian wanting a fuller life, not just to be following her husband's success as a playwright.

K: She says, 'I just don't know what I'm for any more.' I think playwrights were much more spectacular then. Have you read Elizabeth Jane Howard's autobiography? It's called *Slipstream*. It's fascinating. It's very interesting, about the cultural switch between the '50s and '70s. She was married to Kingsley Amis for a long time and before that someone else.

E: How are your daughter's wedding preparations going?

K: The dress is under way anyway. That's a huge, huge relief. But it's so vague.

E: Vague, how?

K: I don't know. It just seems like such an impossibility that my daughter should be getting married. I think I'm stalling somewhere along the line.

E: What, psychologically?

K: I think I am. I think I am.

E: Do you know the ABBA song 'Slipping Through My Fingers'? About a mother watching her little girl walk off to school and sitting down and feeling the loss of her?

K: I shall listen to it as soon as I get home. When children go, it's such a shock. It really was the Lillian moment. 'I don't know what I'm for any more. I just don't know.'

E: So your mum is still around.

K: Oh yeah, very much so. She lives in Wales. She's an extraordinary woman, really is. She would always be hiding somewhere with a book. There were five of us. So I think downtime was probably quite rare. In those days it was easier to read because there wasn't anything else to do. I try and get my youngest son to read now. 'I don't like books.' Whereas my eldest son wanders around with some philosopher in his pocket. He'll grow out of it.

E: He sounds quite sexy, if you don't mind me saying.

K: I think a lot of girls find him sexy. She says, not un-proud. Tell me, do you read the comments that people post online underneath your columns?

---

12. SEXY
—
Earlier this year dating app Tinder tried to identify the 'sexiest jobs' based on the number of 'right swipes' (a gesture denoting interest in an individual) that different profiles receive, and 'philosopher', scandalously, did not rank. The top five results for men and women were:

Men:
1. Pilot
2. Founder/Entrepreneur
3. Firefighter
4. Doctor
5. TV/Radio Personality

Women:
1. Physical Therapist
2. Interior Designer
3. Founder/Entrepreneur
4. PR/Communication
5. Teacher

E: Usually.

K: That was my daughter's job. She was doing the comments on *The New York Times*. She said it was just so depressing, how vicious and mad people are.

E: And just as likely to say something about your hair and tits as they are about the thing you've written.

K: I don't need to know what people say about my hair and tits, thank you very much.

E: No? I could ask that guy there?

K: No, thank you. I'd rather not know. I made the mistake once of seeing a gorgeous picture of yours truly on the internet, and it was some blog saying, 'Oh my God, when is she going to get her hair sorted out?' Suddenly it becomes, 'All my life I thought I was pretty and in fact I'm just a haystack with a face on the front of it.'

E: A haystack? The terrible thing is — and I've noticed it happening to me regarding comments — you realise that your skin is becoming thicker and thicker, which I think is really dangerous.

K: I think it's dangerous in both ways, because people don't care what they say any more. Nothing ever lands. It just...

E: Creates a fog of hatred.

K: Yeah, like a little crust of hatred around the world.

E: What's the answer?

K: Get offline.

E: Do you really think that's it?

K: I think it is. I think that — no, I don't. I think it's impossible.

E: I think it's about creating a better internet. I feel like it's just at the beginning now.

K: Then you hear things about this only being the tip of the iceberg. What you and I look at on the internet is 0.005% of the horrors that are out there. You can buy people and slaves and organs.

E: Can you just give me the...?

K: www.OrgansAreUs.com. Horrible, isn't it?

E: Yes.

K: When you read the comments, you kind of understand why, because there's so much venom.

13. HAYSTACK
—
In 2014, the Italian artist Sven Sachsalber placed a haystack in the Palais de Tokyo gallery in Paris and then deliberately lost a needle in it. To recover the needle took him just under thirty hours, which tells us something about something, surely.

E: Do you google yourself?

K: No, God, never. I mean, only in dire circumstances. At the end of a play I have a look. So type in 'Kristin Scott Thomas *The Audience*' or 'Kristin Scott Thomas...'

E: 'Fabulous'...

K: *'Electra'*.

E: ...'good hair'.

K: No, I mean reviews that I know will be great. Then the first one you will see will be the one from Quentin Letts, the *Daily Mail*, which gives one star — 'Kristen Scott Thomas is ridiculous.' Aren't we meant to be talking about books?

E: OK. Is there another character that you've really identified with and have found yourself through?

K: The boy in *The Goldfinch*. The descriptions of when he goes home to the bombed house, and losing his parents. It just takes me straight back to losing mine. She describes a child's *désaveu*, which is the most fabulous word in French — confusion and dismay, the catastrophe of childhood. She describes it so well. That really got me, that one. Still does.

E: Have you met Donna Tartt?

K: I've said hello to her. She's about this high. She's smaller than her books.

E: Are you in a position where you could get in touch with somebody like that and say, 'I'd like to do a project with you'?

K: I'm not brave enough to do that. I have a great admiration for Martin Amis, and met him at a cocktail party given by my friends at the bookshop. This friend of mine said, 'It would be great to see you in London.' He says, 'Yes, we should all have lunch.' At that moment I just turned my back and walked away. I just couldn't cope with it. Such a fan. I'm terrified of — I think most actors have this thing about being frightened of being found a fraud. I remember I had to write to Jane, to Elizabeth Jane Howard. It took me about a week to compose a letter, because I was just so frightened of writing the wrong thing.

E: Is that because you feel like you're not expected to have a voice?

K: Kind of. But it turned out that Elizabeth Jane Howard wasn't frightening at all. I went to stay with her once. She used to come and see plays that I was in, which I find amazingly flattering. She was incredibly excited about our adaptation. We didn't get the script right before she died, unfortunately. I've made over seventy-something films, but I'm incredibly excited about it and frightened by the whole idea of this one, which is a good thing, I think. Excitement and fright aren't very far apart, are they?

E: That's a good place to end.
    K: It is, isn't it?

EVA WISEMAN is a commissioning editor and columnist on *Observer Magazine* in London, and took the day off to meet Kristin in Paris. She was particularly impressed by the Eurostar toilets, which had a vase of trompe-l'oeil flowers by the soap dispenser, and a small rendering of the *Mona Lisa*.

# PARIS READS

Kristin shared the titles of some favourite purchases from her most cherished Parisian bookshops.

NOTEBOOKS (2005)
Anton Chekhov

From one of the greatest playwrights and short fiction writers of all time, comes this miscellany of 'anything and everything,' says Kristin: odd musings, anecdotes, observations, fragmented ideas and partly-transcribed conversations. Captivating in its ability to communicate the workings of a brilliant, modernist mind, *Notebooks* resemble more 'notes to self' so don't worry if you don't really know what's going on.

SUBMISSION (2015)
Michel Houellebecq

Published only hours before the Charlie Hebdo attacks, *Submission* presents a vision of the not-so-distant future where moderate Muslims govern France. As all women are forced to wear the veil, Jews are urged to 'return' to Israel and an increasing number of Islamic-run countries join the EU, France finds itself once again a political global superpower. Decide for yourself what proportion of satire, prophecy and schadenfreude is being employed by the author.

THE CAT'S TABLE (2011)
Michael Ondaatje

This work of 'fiction' (based on a real voyage by the author) recounts three weeks on an ocean liner from Colombo to England in the 1950s from the point of view of an 11-year-old narrator and two boys he befriends on board. The cast of thieves, adulterers, gamblers, mentors, healers and dreamers they meet will influence the rest of their lives. Kristin bought her copy at the The Village Voice, a favourite bookshop of Ondaatje's that closed in 2012.

JOB (1930)
Joseph Roth

A modern retelling of the Biblical Book of Job, this novel grapples with one of the most difficult of questions for believers and non-believers alike: why do bad things happen to good people? Death, madness and destruction plague the devoutly Jewish Mendel Singer (aka Job), recently emigrated from Tsarist Russia to New York City. Can his faith sustain his pain?

### EVERYTHING RAVAGED, EVERYTHING BURNED (2009)
Wells Tower

Kristin is a fan of Left Bank English-language bookshop Shakespeare and Company, and counts the owner Sylvia Whitman as a close friend. 'She gives me great recommendations, and one I particularly loved was a collection of short stories by this young American writer.' Set (mostly) in contemporary America, these nine short stories paint a rather sorry picture of the male sex — as cheaters, deserters, manipulators, bullies and liars — and will likely leave you feeling a little morose, in the most satisfying way, of course.

### MY BRILLIANT FRIEND (2011)
Elena Ferrante

The first of a feverish quadrilogy by the pseudonymous Italian novelist. Ostensibly the story of a young girl and her friend growing up in Italy in the last century, Ferrante recounts the tribulations of being a woman, a wife and a mother as a country crawls towards modernity. It will keep you awake with its raw, intimate magic and Coppola-esque scale and might.

### POINT OMEGA (2010)
Don DeLillo

Another purchase from Shakespeare and Company, this short novel contains multitudes. Featuring a scholar enlisted to devise an 'intellectual framework', for the Iraq War, DeLillo's sparse, unmistakable prose sculpts an ominous narrative whose title comes from the so-called Omega Point, a zen-like state of divine unification.

### LIEUTENANT GUSTL (1901)
Arthur Schnitzler

Written as an interior monologue, Lieutenant Gustl superbly allegorizes the alternate reality that exists within us all, in parallel with our outward persona and eventual actions. Feelings of dishonour lead the lieutenant to resolve to take his own life only to be spared by good news at the final hour. What happens in between is a mental workout familiar to us all.

### LES ANNEES (2008)
Annie Ernaux

This book only exists *en Français* so get cracking on your Rosetta Stone! Ernaux's lyrical, existential and highly visual novel fluctuates between descriptions of photographs of the narrator taken over nearly sixty years and a specific painting that serves to anchor the narrative. Kristin's copy, bought from an unnamed bookshop 'across the road' is published by Gallimard. 'Their covers are so chic,' she says. 'No pictures, just the title in red.'

# THE HAPPY READER

Pursuing love and preserving sanity in the face of a giant, frightening wilderness: part two of The Happy Reader is obsessed by Willa Cather's heartbreaking epic, O PIONEERS!

Bookish Quarterly — Issue nº 8

"One January day, thirty years ago, the little town of Hanover, anchored on a windy Nebraska tableland, was trying not to be blown away."

**OPENING LINE**
Willa Cather's opening line both sets the scene and establishes the theme of humanity's precariousness — even in what should be a safe haven — when confronted with the elemental forces of the frontier.

INTRODUCTION

Autumn is the season of harvest and this year, in the land that calls it 'fall', it has been backdrop to one of the most dramatic elections ever fought. Our Book of the Season, writes SEB EMINA, is Willa Cather's 1913 novel *O Pioneers!*, a story of human nature, extreme agriculture, and the riskiness of sexual chemistry which tells us a lot about an eternally divided country that may not, deep down, be that divided at all.

# THE PLAINS ARE ENORMOUS

*O Pioneers!* portrays a series of scenes from the fundamental beginnings of the American nation. A boundless, unforgiving wilderness is tamed by the sheer perseverance of the migrant spirit. There is a young rural community, joyous and romantic but riddled with bigotry and stupidity. There is illness, loneliness and death. There is also fruit, dancing and ducks. Against this backdrop, love stories play out, the kind that, throughout human history — in the words of one of Willa Cather's eternally striving loners — 'go on repeating themselves as fiercely as if they had never happened before, like the larks in this country, that have been singing the same five notes over for thousands of years.'

Actually, despite its primordial atmosphere, *O Pioneers!* is set little more than a century ago. In the 1900s, pioneers from Sweden, France, Germany and Bohemia were out there still, struggling to build something on the wild darkness of the so-called Great Plains (between the Rocky Mountains and the Mississippi River), on unmapped territories where people were prone to be driven by loneliness into a delirium known as 'prairie madness'. At its centre is Alexandra Bergson, who we meet as a teenager in the remote town of Hanover, Nebraska. Alexandra's father, who brought the family over from Sweden, is dying. He intends to leave the ailing farm in Alexandra's hands as, unlike his two eldest sons, she is a born farmer. He dies, she takes over. Against all received wisdom, when other pioneering farmers give up and leave, she not only clings on but borrows more money to buy more land, a gamble that pays off incredibly. Rattling around in the background is her mother, who likes to make preserves, but never really says much, and dies between two of the chapters.

As a woman taking on what was typically a man's role, Alexandra is Cather-ish to the core. Just like her heroine, the author had both a conservative world-view and a tendency to shrug off society's expectations of womanhood. Cather liked to wear masculine clothing; as a student at the University of Nebraska, she sported a military-style short haircut and went by the nickname 'William'. Although she neither labelled her sexuality nor allowed others to do so, she formed a series of close relationships with women and spent the last thirty-nine years of her life living with the editor Edith Lewis.

It's tempting to see Alexandra as living a life that Cather felt she might have had. The author's family had lived in the same valley in Virginia for six generations, and then left for Nebraska when she was nine years old. She fell in love with her new home but her career as a writer inadvertently propelled her towards cities of increasing sizes: Lincoln, Pittsburgh and eventually, inevitably, New York. Alexandra, on the other hand, stays. By the end of *O Pioneers!* she is seemingly as much a part of the landscape of her childhood as the ponds or the trees. Another character, meanwhile, lives in New York for a while,

and finds it to have its own version of prairie madness: 'All we have ever managed to do is to pay our rent, the exorbitant rent that one has to pay for a few square feet of space near the heart of things. We live in the streets, in the parks, in the theatres. We sit in restaurants and concert halls and look about at the hundreds of our own kind and shudder.'

Today's Manhattanites will wonder what's changed. As will anyone trying, as so many are, to understand the complicated relationship between the US's cities and its so-called heartland. Cather wrote a novel about a very specific place at a very specific time, but its continued resonance far beyond the Nebraskan flatlands, a hundred and three years after it original publication, shows her metaphor about the larks singing the same notes again and again, from one century to the next, really did have something to it.

---

COMMUNICATION

The exclamation mark, writes JOHN SELF, may be the most abused of punctuation options, but it has a definite magic when it turns up in a title.

# HELLO THERE!

The first significant encounter for a reader of *O Pioneers!* — before they even become a reader — is with the exclamation mark at the end of its title. Lying in wait, there it is! Instantly it suggests a book that will be dramatic, ironic, humorous, exciting. Pretty eloquent for a symbol that, when I was a boy hammering out letters to authors on an Olivetti typewriter twenty-five years ago, didn't even have its own key, but had to be conjured up with *full stop > backspace > apostrophe*.

The origin of the exclamation mark is unclear, if you discard the too-cute-to-be-plausible suggestion that it started as a stylisation of *io*, a Latin expression of joy. It is a symbol that makes no sound of its own but changes how we read what comes before it, and its versatility has given it many names. In John Hart's 1551 essay *The Opening of the Unreasonable Writing of Our Inglish Toung*, it was 'the wonderer', while Thomas Coar's *A Grammar of the English Tongue* (1796) called it the 'note of admiration' ('placed after an interjection, and such words as express wonder, as Alas! O times! O manners!'). More colloquially — more *exclamation-markly* — it's been known as the bang, shriek or screamer, often by professional deployers such as printers and journalists.

Willa Cather took *her* use from Walt Whitman, whose poem 'Pioneers! O Pioneers!' went one exclamation further. Giving the title of your piece of writing its own punctuation is a very fancy treat. It can give rise to excitable-sounding commentary ('I love *O Pioneers!*! What do you think of *O Pioneers!*?'), but it certainly makes a book stand out. Its addition can achieve a surprising range of effects:

1. POEM
—
From 'Pioneers! O Pioneers':

From Nebraska, from Arkansas, / Central inland race are we, from Missouri, with the continental blood intervein'd; / All the hands of comrades clasping, all the Southern, all the Northern, / Pioneers! O pioneers!

*What a Carve Up!* — In this satire of British society and politics, the exclamation mark rightly suggests chaos and outrage. Jonathan Coe took his title from a 1961 British comedy-horror film. This is because exclamation-marked titles are so rare they need to be reused.

*Westward Ho!* — A declarative, imperative tone for Charles Kingsley's 1855 novel (the first to use an exclamation mark in the name). Westward Ho! was also recycled, as the name of a *(continues on page 39)*

seaside village in Devon, in the belief that naming it after a bestselling book would 'excite increased public attention'.

*Absalom, Absalom!* — William Faulkner, Southern disintegration, incest, unreliable narrative: frankly, that single exclamation mark seems restrained.

*Make Room! Make Room!* — There's distress in the screaming title of Harry Harrison's prescient 1966 novel about overpopulation, which inspired the movie *Soylent Green,* though (spoiler alert!) the famous plot twist doesn't feature in the book.

*One is Fun!* — The exclamation mark in the title of Delia Smith's 1986 cookery book for 'solo dining' smacks of desperate pleading. Recipes include brown kidney soup, liver with sherry sauce and 'individual Alpine egg' (ingredients: egg, grated cheese).

Clearly we need more book titles with exclamation marks. Indeed, there are many existing titles out there, pitifully naked, which would surely benefit from one: *Disgrace!*, *Jude the Obscure!*, *What Maisie Saw!*, *To the Lighthouse!*, *Housekeeping!*, *Of Mice and Men!*, *Crime and Punishment!*, *As You Like It!*.

But let's not take this expansion of exclamation marks too far. In Padget Powell's *The Interrogative Mood*, every sentence ends with a question mark. Let's hope nobody does the same with exclamation marks! If they haven't already! Can you imagine how annoying that would be!

JOHN SELF is a book reviewer who lives in Belfast. His favourite punctuation mark is the em dash, because it conveys such a sense of — of — well —

2. DELIA SMITH
—
The UK's bestselling cookery author is also, with her husband Michael Wynn-Jones, the owner of a football team, namely Norwich City FC – aka 'the canaries'.

---

TRAVEL

What happens when you read a novel in the place in which it is set? Does the landscape seem different somehow? Do the words on the page? Starting in the small towns of Nebraska, CLANCY MARTIN drags his daughters along on an *O Pioneers!*-powered road trip.

# EXCITING, EMPTY ROAD

When our silver PT Cruiser started smoking outside Beatrice, Nebraska, I knew the ghost of Willa Cather had plans for us. We had driven through 'the little town of Hanover', as Cather describes it in the opening sentence of *O Pioneers!*, without even noticing, despite the fact that I had two earnest navigators happily operating their iPhones.

In *O Pioneers!* everyone is always travelling, as you might expect: to pioneer, says the *Oxford English Dictionary*, is 'to prepare, clear, open up (a wayroad)'. Characters ride horses, hitch buggies, mount carriages, drive wagons, and of course walk, such as Alexander and Marie who follow a wedding procession on foot, 'each leading a cow'. But generally speaking they don't go very far, and often their short journeys end in disaster, and I was concerned that our fate had become linked to the novel. I had considered going to explore

Cather country on my own, but pioneering is a family business, and since my girls were on summer break and we had a family invitation in Dallas, I decided to use the opportunity to investigate several of the great plain states of America. We were out of the low wet country of Missouri and up into the high yellow plains of Nebraska. Kansas, Oklahoma and Texas were next on the list. We'd return through the rolling low mountains of Arkansas. That was the plan.

'Siri, where is Hanover?' This was Portia, my nine-year-old.

Siri: 'Here's Hannover, Germany.'

Siri had repeatedly tried to send us overseas. The towns in Nebraska were settled by Nordic people: Swedes, northern Germans, Danes. So Siri had developed the idea that we were somewhere near the Baltic.

Cather's Hanover may be an entirely fictional place: scholars have argued that she invented it. But the real Hanover, Nebraska, is not far from Red Cloud, where she grew up, so we were determined to see it.

'I'm looking at Google Maps,' Margaret, my eleven-year-old, said. 'I think you need to turn around. Dad, what's wrong with the car?'

Clouds of radiator-fluid vapour poured abundantly from the hood. The car steamed often, and I could see the road reasonably well, but it was a bit alarming. Also, Margaret has a fear of car fires that developed when we once had a Range Rover burst into flame on I-70 in Kansas City. I've had bad luck with car radiators all of my adult life, probably because I've lived in hot places — Texas, Kansas, Missouri — and tend to buy cheap, used cars.

'She's just a little hot. I need to put some water in her, and maybe some more radiator fluid. I'll pull over at the first gas station.'

It was early evening and I had begun to accept that we wouldn't make it back up to (the real) Hanover that night. We were only two days into our journey and suddenly I felt defeated. 'A golden afterglow throbbed in the west, but the country already looked empty and mournful.' I needed to find a motel.

'Let's get some dinner. See if you can find us a hotel, Portia.'

'The AmericInn Lodge has a pool.'

'Let me see,' Margaret said. 'That's in Lincoln,' she said dismissively. Then she added: 'Dad, can we stay there? It looks really nice in the pictures.'

I stopped at a little local gas station that had a hose outside. Once we were inside, while the girls looked for Toxic Waste and new flavours of Nerds, I saw they sold bait and tackle: live fish swam in big water coolers and fat sad red and black earthworms squirmed in smaller ones. A fisherman's stop, so I asked the fellow working there if he could tell me where I might find Norway Creek, because I wanted to see if there was any chance that 'Alexandra's house' and the 'tall osage orange hedges' surrounding it actually existed. The man who ran the gas station and the other people we had seen, in their trucks, in the restaurants and convenience stores, were tall, sturdy, square-featured, Scandinavian stock, just the people you expect to see in Nebraska, clear descendants of Cather's pioneers. I could imagine the impressive white wooden farmhouse with the flower gardens, walnut trees and beehives she described. Alexandra is the heart of the novel, the pioneer who actually creates something for her family — she is a character straight out of a Chekhov play, with her lonely, moralising and earnest celebration of 'the land' and hard work — and I wanted to see what that farm might have looked like.

The fellow who owned the gas station was himself a fisherman and knew about Norway Creek. He gave me directions to a town called Superior. 'If you're headed to Hanover you're going the right direction. Good fishing. Bass, blue gill, golden shiner, crappie.'

Hanover is a township of about a hundred people — not much more than a church, a gas station, some side roads leading to small, ranch-style housing developments, and a romantic red railroad station next to old tracks. I was focused on the telephone poles, because the night before, while the girls played in the indoor pool at the hotel in Lincoln, I read to them aloud my favourite scene from the novel: the opening, when Emil, only five, is crying in the snow because his kitten has climbed up a telegraph pole in the fierce cold of January, and his sister Alexandra saves the kitten by recruiting her best friend, Carl. 'Only you must stop crying,' Alexandra tells her tender-hearted little brother, 'or I won't move a step.'

Image: © Andrew Moore / Gallery Stock

# O PIONEERS!

**BIRD'S EYE**
A set of amazing aerial photographs of the Great Plains states (also see p. 33, 59) with only small traces of humanity visible.

Visitors are welcome at Willa Cather's childhood home in Red Cloud, Nebraska.

'Dad, it's a hundred degrees out here. All we've done today is sweat. Can we please get in the car?'

'I'm letting the car cool down. The air conditioning isn't working anyway.'

There were no people in the street. I was humming 'mad dogs and Englishmen go out in the midday sun', and thinking that the Nebraska winters made much more of an impression on Cather than the summers. Part III of the novel is called 'Winter Memories' and it opens with one of the nicest paragraphs of description in all of her work, in which:

> Winter has settled down over the Divide again; the season in which Nature recuperates, in which she sinks to sleep between the fruitfulness of autumn and the passion of spring. The birds have gone. The teeming life that goes on down in the long grass is exterminated.

Spring is celebrated in the novel; the tone, overall, is autumnal; but never do you hear about what I was feeling as I walked between telephone poles: the sun flattening you like an iron on the gravel. Weirdly, in a novel that features weather and farming so prominently, no one ever complains about the heat.

In Red Cloud we toured Cather's quaint, tiny brown childhood home with its white picket fence; we drove by the beautiful old train depot and the opera house; we drove out of town, sat on the stone bench at the Cather memorial prairie and stared at the long, low hills, still green in the merciless August sun (it had been a wet summer); and we never found Norway Creek, though we did see Crooked Creek and the large white farmhouse just outside Superior, Nebraska, that I thought might have impressed itself upon the young author's mind.

'We drove for three days so you could see a white house. There are like a hundred of those in our neighbourhood in Kansas City. It's not even nice.'

'You're right. Let's go. Onward ho.'

'What does that even mean?'

We were back on I-35, the highway I'm doomed to traverse throughout my adult life. Twenty-one, working at a jewellery store in Arlington, Texas, and dating a woman at Baylor University: I-35. Twenty-three, going to graduate school in Austin: I-35. Twenty-five, driving with my new wife and my dad to St Olaf, where I was working on my dissertation, and then on to Winnipeg, where he grew up: I-35. Twenty-seven, driving to Dallas to open my own chain of jewellery stores: I-35. Thirty, back in graduate school, driving to see a woman — my second wife — in Oklahoma City: I-35. Thirty-three, driving from Austin, Texas, to Lawrence, Kansas, to take my first job as a professor: I-35. And now here I am, nearly fifty, driving from Kansas City to Lincoln to Wichita to Oklahoma City and down to Dallas, on I-35. The landscape looks the same everywhere on I-35: it is often beautiful country, plains stretching out to the horizon,

Image: © Michael Christopher Brown / Magnum Photos

frequently rolling in low hills; you see hawks, kestrels, even eagles; cows, sheep, horses, farmhouses, mysterious little dirt roads, small lakes, old trucks raising dust in the distance, tractors; and also, of course, billboards, strip malls, roadside gas stations, motels and restaurants. I am Canadian, but for thirty years I've lived in the US, have driven through every state except for Maine and Alaska, most of them several times, and can say with confidence that if you want to see the heartland of America, the most honest way to do it is to drive I-35.

We were out of Arkansas, halfway through Kansas, about three hours from Oklahoma City. Twenty or so fifty-foot-tall, three-bladed white windmills turned slowly in the still summer air.

'What are they, Dad?'

'It's a wind farm. They make electricity.'

The light steel windmills tremble throughout their frames and tug at their moorings, as they vibrate in the wind that often blows from one week's end to another across that high, active, resolute stretch of country.

The car was overheating again, but then it rained, everything cooled, and we drove through the storm past Wichita, across the border, and into Oklahoma City, when the sun reappeared. Then, after lunch at a place called Johnny's Hamburgers on Britton Road, while sitting in a line of traffic watching an endless line of railway cars passing by, the engine exploded.

There were no flames this time, but my daughters were panicking and we hustled out of the car. A kind, tall, square-shouldered Oklahoman, very German-looking, a Bayern type, with an accent so strong I couldn't understand him — 'Ya-ull-hassumm-ah-nj-en-trubuhl' — let the girls stand in his air-conditioned sign-and-print shop while we got the car off the road and called a tow truck. As I write this, a month later, my poor beloved silver PT Cruiser is still sitting in the parking lot at a Pep Boys in 'The Village', North Oklahoma City, on Memorial Drive. Four to six thousand dollars in estimated repairs to a car that was worth about twenty-five hundred. I've called a salvage company, and they are paying me three hundred as soon as I FedEx the keys and title.

'Dad, do we have to go home?'

'No, no, we're not letting a little thing like our car dying stop us.'

We rented a red Jeep Patriot — it was comfortable, and seemed to fit the theme — and soon we were back on I-35.

As we came down out of the Ozark Mountains — they call them mountains because they are in the flatland of Oklahoma, but they are really more like modest hills with some boulders — into the long, dirty, wide breadth of northern Texas, we saw ranches on both sides of us with horses and cattle, a Native American casino and, in the distance, another wind farm. I thought of Alexandra walking with Carl at the end of the novel, tired but reconciled with the life she had made for herself in the plains. I thought about how familiar everything looked to me, how much this country, such as it was, had become my home. I told my daughters, 'Well, here comes Texas,' and they both looked up from their phones for a second to say, 'Yay!'

They paused on the last ridge of the pasture, overlooking the house and the windmill and the stables that marked the site of John Bergson's homestead. On every side brown waves of the earth rolled away to meet the sky.

That is just what it looked like. Yellow and brown waves of plain and earth rolling away on either side of us until they met the sky. And I thought, You know, this is what my home looks like. When my daughters have kids, and they come back to the middle of the country, they will think, this is home.

Then they went back to their video games, and I looked for the next Love's Travel Stop, so that we could pull over and buy some beef jerky.

CLANCY MARTIN is a writer and philosophy professor who lives with his wife and daughters in Kansas City, Missouri. As a pioneer-in-training, he once drove twenty-eight hours — without stopping to sleep — from his father's hospital bed in Miami, Florida, to his girlfriend's trailer home in Waco, Texas, whereupon, at 4am in the morning, he was shot at (with an old hunting rifle) by his girlfriend's roommate (she missed).

Author YELENA MOSKOVICH examines the multitudinal talents of Nebraskan pageant winners.

# MISS NEBRASKA

**3. MARY LEE JEPSEN**
—
Crowned Miss Nebraska 1962 following her 'Ritual Fire Dance'.

**4. TERESA SCANLAN**
—
Nebraska's sole Miss America won the day with her piano virtuosity.

Since its beginnings in Atlantic City in 1921, the Miss America competition has had each state, including Nebraska, sending along the ambassadors of their most innovative charisma. As the 'American Experiment' nation continued to try things out, so have those crowned Miss Nebraska pioneered a series of skill-sets that echo the country's quirk for stylized ingenuity.

Whereas initial pageant contestants pursued the crown with bombastic displays, Diana Louise Hann won the 1953 Miss Nebraska title with a quieter approach, listing her talent as 'Art' and exhibiting portraitures and still lifes. The same year, Americans became the first people in the world to perceive televised hues, as colour TV sets were released into the market.

In 1962, Miss Nebraska unexpectedly hailed bravado over ballad, crowning the charming daredevil, 18-year-old Mary Lee Jepsen for her 'Ritual Fire Dance' where she twirled three fire batons during an acrobatics routine. A month later, Paul Neal 'Red' Adair, famed Texan fire-fighter, tackled and put out a 450 foot pillar of flame, nicknamed the Devil's Cigarette Lighter, that had been burning for over five months in a gas field in the Algerian Sahara.

As women's liberation activists picketed 1968's Miss America event, an alternative state pageant promoting Nebraska's beef cattle industry crowned Ann Coffee as 'Miss Nebraska Stock Grower'. Coffee traded the traditional bouquet for a human-sized cut of locally grown beef, and the winning photo was made into promotional postcards.

The 1974 Miss Nebraska competition prized Sharon Sue Pelc's ventroloquised act of the nostalgic tune 'Those Were the Days'. Shortly after, news buzzed over the invention of the artificial cough by an American surgeon, known as the re-animating Heimlich Manouever.

In the 21st century, attention turned to preservation. In 2010, two buildings by the monumental American architect Louis I Kahn were restored as Teresa Scanlan became the youngest ever Miss Nebraska at seventeen. She won the crown with her piano rendition of 'White Water Chopped Sticks' by Calvin Jones, while revealing special affinity for making clothes out of duct tape. 'I was home-schooled my whole entire life, and then my last year of high school, I went to the public high school and wore my duct-tape clothing.' Following her state title, Scanlan not only went on to become the first Miss Nebraska to win Miss America, but was also featured in the eighth Annual Avon Heritage Duct Tape Festival.

YELENA MOSKOVICH is a Ukrainian-born Midwestern author living in Paris. Her debut novel is *The Natashas* (Serpent's Tail 2016). She studied playwriting at Emerson College, the Lecoq School of Physical Theatre, and Université Paris 8. Her plays have been produced in the US, Vancouver, Paris, and Stockholm.

O PIONEERS!

Postcard featuring Ann Coffee, 1968's Miss Nebraska Stock Grower.

The world's most famous conspiracy theorist bellows out an earthy list of manly traits. It becomes a viral sensation and shows, writes ALEXANDER ZAITCHIK, how the world of online opinion has become the fizzing frontier of our new, media-encircled reality.

# POST-FACTUAL PIONEER

On 4 July 2016, the radio host Alex Jones treated viewers and listeners to one of his episodic eruptions. The Texas-based Jones has made the public rant, a rhetorical mode associated with wild-eyed street-corner paranoia, into a cornerstone of Infowars, his multi-million-dollar internet-and-radio media empire. But even by his usual standards, this was special.

His face red, his shirt white, his blazer blue, the barrel-chested Jones let rip, a wild look on his face. 'I'm a *pioneer*!' he snarled, and then: 'I'm an *explorer*! I'm a *human* and I'm *comin*'! My heart's *big*. It's got hot *blood* running through it *fast*. I like to *fight*, too. I like to *eat*. I like to *have children*. I'm *here*. I got a *life force*! This is a *human*. *This* is what we *look like*. This is what we *act like*. This is what *everybody* was like *before us*. This is what I *am*. I'm a *throwback*. I'm *here*. I've got the *fire of human liberty*. I'm settin' fires *everywhere*!' He stopped, eyes glaring, and took a deep breath before going to a commercial break filled with Infowars-endorsed health products and survival goods.

At the dawn of the Obama era, Jones was unknown outside of transatlantic conspiracy subculture. Today, at its sunset, Jones is a character commanding such recognition you could imagine him getting a *Simpsons* cameo. When this guttural roar about liberty-loving manhood went viral, it did so with the familiarity of celebrity. The website of *Esquire* magazine asked, as if they'd been following him forever, 'Is this the best Alex Jones Freakout of All Time?'

Millions have watched Jones' rise to prominence with bemused fascination. This lens darkened as Jones aligned himself with another figure known for generating bemused fascination, Donald Trump. During the election campaign, Jones promoted Trump and his surrogates (and was in turn praised by the candidate on the show). More importantly, Jones provided Trump's campaign with the runaway 'Hillary for Prison' meme. This led many to take serious notice of him for the first time, and ask, 'Who is this guy?'

A good place to start is the word he used to start his rant: 'pioneer'. Jones' Texas roots stretch back to literal pioneers. His ancestors on both sides settled the western frontier during the early nineteenth century, near what later became Houston. One of these lines, Jones told me years ago over burritos in downtown Austin, produced a martyr at the Alamo. Of all the characters that populated that dusty world, it's not the tobacco-spitting coonskin-capped Davy Crockett that Jones most evokes, but the Methodist preachers of the Second Great Awakening who spread a fiery gospel across the ranches and two-horse towns of the independent Republic of Texas.

5. AUSTIN
—
Many assert that the best burritos in Austin, Texas are found at Cabo Bob's, and will specifically point to the brisket and queso variety.

# O PIONEERS!

Alex Jones is a pioneer. He likes to eat. He likes to have children.

These preachers, known as 'circuit riders', roamed the frontier with throats full of fire and brimstone. Their intensity was famous back east, where people associated these horseback Methodists with insanity. They railed against fashionable secular trends and warned of the devil tempting Americans to turn their backs to God, as Jones does today. In Jones' telling, Barack Obama has been a 'wicked, wicked devil' sending the world to hell under the co-direction of 'globalist goblins'. Every Sunday, Alex Jones attends a Methodist service with his family.

Jones, meanwhile, is a pioneer of the modern variety — a multi-platform crossover act melding conspiracy, politics and entertainment, whose ideological frontier was settled 150 years after the heyday of the circuit riders in a regional phenomenon known as 'Alt Texas'. This mini cultural renaissance took place during the 1980s and 1990s; Houston and Austin were its twin capitals. In film, Alt Texas produced Richard Linklater and Robert Rodriguez. In comedy, it produced the anti-establishment rant-comedy of Bill Hicks and Sam Kinison (the latter worked as a travelling scam-preacher before finding fame as a comic), both of whom exerted great influence on the teenage Alex Jones.

When Hicks died in 1994 at the age of thirty-two, Jones was a rising star at Austin Access, the local public-access TV station that served as a creative base for a generation of south Texas musicians, directors and comedians. During their years of overlap, Hicks grew increasingly interested in conspiracy theories, and performed material about the JFK assassination, NAFTA and the siege at Waco. He lambasted the growing power of banks and corporations, sometimes declaring, 'Twenty-two families control everything!' Following Hicks' death, Jones adopted these themes as the basis of his daily radio show.

More recently, Jones has amped up the hyper-masculine edge to his act. The 'I'm a pioneer!' rant was a dramatic example of this, and it may not be long before Jones rips out a zebra's throat with his teeth live in his studio. In Jones' sexually charged New World Order narrative, tyranny is synonymous with passivity and feminisation; it is the submission and enslavement of the American male. Jones often depicts globalists and their liberal media allies as whispering in effeminate 'NPR voices', pushing unmanly cultural trends towards the ultimate goal of a post-gender dystopia where men have lisps and the frogs are gay.

There is a theory on the internet that Bill Hicks faked his own death and created Alex Jones as a posthumous performance-art project. If so, Hicks-as-Jones has proven a master at manipulating the new media landscape, where viral content is king. Jones was an internet pioneer who early understood its potential — for bypassing terrestrial radio, for posting short clips — better and before his peers. His YouTube archive is on track to hit 1 billion views sometime in 2017. How many will it take to spark Jones' 'wildfires of human liberty'? Who knows. But there's no denying that when Jones lets out his broadcasting kraken, when he's really feeling the spirit, even his harshest critics become strangely hypnotised. Jones might claim he's a 'throwback' to some golden age of hot-blooded manhood. This might be one of the conceits undergirding his success. But the truth is he's leading his industry and his country into the angry, conspiracy-tinged, infotainment world unfolding around us, and has been for a long time.

ALEXANDER ZAITCHIK is a freelance journalist and the author of two books, most recently, *The Gilded Rage: A Wild Ride through Donald Trump's America*. His favourite Alex Jones conspiracy-rant involves globalists smoking DMT to receive instructions from inter-dimensional elves.

---

FOOD

Few foods come more heavily laden with psychological baggage than a jar of home-made pickles or preserves. A shelf of these multicoloured memory-caskets, says food writer BEE WILSON, can be either twee or punk, and can speak of both old-fashioned survivalism and modish sophistication.

# PRESERVERANCE

Want to show you have old-fashioned survival skills? Bring out the pickle jars. During this year's US presidential campaign, Hillary Clinton countered rumours about her health by opening a jar of pickles with her bare hands in the middle of an interview on the Jimmy Kimmel show. Fighting fit! Of course this was done partly — partly — in jest, but the joke only worked because pickles, and their parent category of preserves, remain such a powerful symbol of self-reliance. Preserved goods are the food of pioneers. They are there in *O Pioneers!*, with Alexandra's mother displaying a positive 'mania' for creating them. The old Swedish woman roams the prairie looking for any wild fruits — 'fox grapes', 'goose plums', the 'rank buffalo pea' — that she can boil up with sugar. The results are a bit heartbreaking. The rationale is to provide the family with a source of winter calories, but in truth she makes preserves more for psychological reasons than culinary ones: the sheer amount of sugar required for all these jams is a drain on the household finances. Mrs Bergson's preserves reassure her that in this godforsaken, inhospitable landscape, she is still civilised.

The urge to preserve has never been strictly logical. These days, it is less so than ever. In an era of fridges and readily available Bonne Maman, preserving is less about survival and more about make-believe. I doubt we'll ever eat the jars of green tomato chutney we have left over from my bout of overenthusiastic pickling a few years ago. We almost never eat the kinds of meal where green tomato chutney is required, something I might have considered before I got carried away and made three litres of the stuff. Not having an orchard or an allotment, jam making also gives me mixed feelings. To use vast amounts of sugar to 'preserve' shop-bought fruit to which I have no personal connection seems an exercise in artifice.

A better argument for pickling and preserving in modern life is not to make food last so much as to transform its flavour. At this year's Oxford Symposium on Food and Cookery, a young chef called Thom Eagle, of Darsham Nurseries, spoke of using pickles as a way to 'salvage flavour from rubbish', of taking cavolo nero stalks and fermenting them with salt 'to an almost truffle-like pungency' in a kind of improvised kimchee.

Preserving is shedding its Women's Institute connotations. To ferment your own sauerkraut and dehydrate your own foraged mushrooms is, today, nigh-on edgy. On a recent trip to Copenhagen, I was struck by the way in which, in the various new-wave Nordic restaurants, it is now virtually compulsory to display a row of beautiful Mason jars filled with various ferments and pickles: a plain wooden shelf at Bror, run by two former sous-chefs from Noma, houses transparent containers of varying sizes inside which lurk murky-green moss, elderflowers, bright pink rose petals, cucumbers and rosehips. The row of jars comes across as a statement of the kitchen's seriousness.

Yet the appeal of preserves is still mostly symbolic. It is ourselves we are preserving. Things in jars exert an extraordinary emotional attachment. Preserves anchor us to the past, to our own past and to a more distant one where all those pioneers knew what to do with a funnel and a long preserving spoon. You spend a fortune on labels and jelly bags and thermometers, all to reassure yourself that you are not the kind of person who needs to buy stuff.

You do not have to eat a preserve to be comforted by it. In fact, it's better in a way if those jars are left unopened, indefinitely, in readiness. In a recent book titled *Batch*, the Canadian couple Joel MacCharles and Dana Harrison write about laying down 300 jars of food in just six months. They don't reveal how two people could possibly get through so many preserves. Their store cupboard is a pickling

The US pickled gherkin market is both huge and stable.

cornucopia, with salted citrus, jams galore, neat rows of pressure-canned asparagus. I desperately wish I had all this, even though I don't much care for canned asparagus. It's the concept that's appealing. To own such a larder is to reassure yourself that whatever horrors might lie ahead, you are prepared.

Incidentally, if you've ever opened a pickle jar you know you don't actually need strong hands to open one. Just bang the edge of the lid forcefully on a table or chopping board and it pops right open.

BEE WILSON is a food writer and historian. Her most recent book was *First Bite: How We Learn to Eat* (Fourth Estate). Looking back, she told THR, the last time she fully felt like a pioneer was when she was seven, a time when every day she would pioneer something such as a new swimming stroke or a new way to spread butter or hit conkers. The only time she gets glimmers of that pioneer freedom now is when she cooks or writes.

---

ENCOUNTER

Eleven decades ago, a young Willa Cather took a ship to England on what was essentially a fan's pilgrimage. But the saying 'you should never meet your heroes', finds CHARLIE CONNELLY, has rarely been truer than of the cringeworthy encounter that ensued with the poet A. E. Housman.

# WILLA'S WANDERS

The heavy pink heads of the rose bushes droop drowsily in the summer heat beneath the ground-floor windows of 17 North Road in Highgate, north London. The front door is white and freshly painted, the lawn lush and well tended. Other than the large green wheelie bin stationed in the gateway, the view is almost identical to the one that greeted Willa Cather 114 years earlier at the end of a long pilgrimage from western Pennsylvania.

The only major change to the house that Cather surveyed on another hot day, in July 1902, is the blue plaque placed beside the front door noting that A. E. Housman wrote *A Shropshire Lad* while living in the two rooms he rented here. Housman, a brilliant classical scholar, had published his lyrical cycle of sixty-three poems in 1896, and by 1902 its poignant evocation of doomed rural youth was resonating hugely with a British public anxiously following the progress of the Second Boer War (the poem would go on to become almost a national epic during the global conflicts of the twentieth century). Willa Cather already knew *A Shropshire Lad* intimately, and that its author resided in the neatly kept suburban villa in front of her. Indeed, it's precisely why she'd crossed an ocean to stand at the end of this very path in order to meet the man arguably most responsible for waking the landscape-inspired writer within her.

Cather was twenty-eight years old when she turned up at Mrs Hunter's boarding house hoping to meet her forty-three-year-old literary hero. *O Pioneers!* was still a decade away; her first poetry collection, *April Twilights*, would be published a year hence. She'd just completed her first year of teaching English and Latin at a Pittsburgh high school after five years of editing the women's periodical *Home Monthly* when she decided to cross the Atlantic and see for herself the land of *A Shropshire Lad* — 'the remoteness, the *(continued on page 54)*

## WILLA

Wilella Cather, who later answered to 'Willa', was born on 7 December 1873. She went on to write twelve novels, three of which — *O Pioneers!*, *The Song of the Lark* and *My Ántonia* — formed the much-revered Prairie Trilogy. Lines from Cather's writing have become a mainstay of online quote aggregators, the most popular being 'that is happiness; to be dissolved into something complete and great', a line about death that is inscribed on her headstone in New Hampshire.

# A SPOTTER'S GUIDE TO THE

☐ **PRAIRIE BARN**
*(Horreum pratensis)*

*Appearance*: Among the largest of the barns. Often red exterior with long sloping gambrel rooflines and gabled doors.
*Smell*: Lofty woody aroma intermingled with horse.
*Habitat*: Common across Nebraska and the whole of north America. Numerous on open grassy plains.
*Size*: 1755cm
*Contents*: Livestock, hay, wedding parties.

☐ **LONG-BILLED CURLEW**
*(Numenius americanus)*

*Appearance*: Very long decurved bill. Feathers are mottled cinnamon above; buffy below.
*Call*: Loud ascending 'cur-lee'.
*Habitat*: Sandy grassland with slopes. Common summer resident in western part of state.
*Size*: 58cm
*Diet*: Crabs and other invertebrates. Known to occasionally eat the eggs of other birds.

☐ **ROUND BARN**
*(Aedificium circus)*

*Appearance*: Circular or polygonal structure, typically with large silo in the centre extending through roof.
*Smell*: A strong methane tang.
*Habitat*: Once frequent across the Midwest especially in Shaker communities. Now increasingly rare.
*Size*: 1200cm
*Contents*: Cattle and grain.

☐ **TURKEY VULTURE**
*(Cathartes aura)*

*Appearance*: Dark brown with red unfeathered head. Will defecate on its own legs to help cool itself down.
*Call*: Usually silent, but may hiss and fight over coveted animal carcasses.
*Habitat*: Open plains and sandhills with ample opportunity for carrion foraging. Common across Nebraska in spring.
*Size*: 69cm
*Diet*: Carrion.

☐ **RING-NECKED DUCK**
*(Aythya collaris)*

*Appearance*: Black back and breast, gray-white stripe on sides, blue bill with two white bars and a black tip.
*Call*: Usually silent, but males will give a soft whistle during courtship.
*Habitat*: Use large lakes and reservoirs during migration. Common across Nebraska in spring and autumn.
*Size*: 43cm
*Diet*: Dive for pondweed, hornwort and snails.

☐ **BANK BARN**
*(Habitaculum obliquus)*

*Appearance*: Hillside construction notable for accessibility of both lower and upper floors from the ground.
*Smell*: Damp sweetness of drying bales and the phenolic notes of a bridle.
*Habitat*: The undulating southeastern counties of Nebraska.
*Size*: 780cm
*Contents*: Draft animals and green hay left to cure.

# BIRDS AND BARNS OF NEBRASKA

☐ **PRAIRIE FALCON**
*(Falco mexicanus)*

*Appearance*: Light brown above, cream-coloured below with heavy spotting. Bathes in dust.
*Call*: Loud '*kree-kree-kree*'.
*Habitat*: Fond of open grassland near to cliffs and rocky outcrops. Breeds in the western part of Nebraska, rare visitor in the East.
*Size*: 45cm
*Diet*: Mostly small mammals and small to medium-sized birds. Have been known to take larger birds such as geese.

☐ **POTATO BARN**
*(Tectum tuberosa)*

*Appearance*: Narrow proportioned triangular prism. Often partly underground with ample ventilation.
*Smell*: Geosmin and petrichor.
*Habitat*: Fields with well drained, loose soil. Rare in Nebraska but found intermittently.
*Size*: 450cm
*Contents*: Potatoes.

☐ **GREATER PRAIRIE-CHICKEN**
*(Tympanuchus cupido)*

*Appearance*: Stocky, with short tail feathers
*Call*: Courting males emit a deep '*oo-loo-woo*' sound known as booming.
*Habitat*: Like undisturbed prairie. Will avoid nesting within a quarter-mile of powerlines. Common in the Nebraskan Sandhills.
*Size*: 43cm
*Diet*: Leaves, seeds, grains, fruits, insects.

☐ **WESTERN MEADOWLARK**
*(Sturnella neglecta)*

*Appearance*: Black v-shaped breast band on yellow underparts. Upperparts are brown with dusky edges.
*Call*: Bubbling, flutelike notes punctuated by a low, explosive '*chuck*'.
*Habitat*: Tall mixed-grass prairies and meadows. Winters in South Nebraska.
*Size*: 22cm
*Diet*: Primarily insects but also seeds and berries.

☐ **SANDHILL CRANE**
*(Grus canadensis)*

*Appearance*: Long legs and neck. Ash-coloured plumage with red cap on forehead. Flies with legs and neck outstretched.
*Call*: Loud rattling '*gar-oo-oo*'.
*Habitat*: Slow moving rivers with sandbars for nesting. Particularly common in spring along Platte Valley.
*Size*: 104cm
*Diet*: Highly varied with berries, small mammals, insects, snails, reptiles, and amphibians all consumed.

☐ **DOUBLE CRIB BARN**
*(Dilectus silvestris)*

*Appearance*: Fashioned from unchinked logs. Two berths separated by a breezeway and connected by the same roof.
*Smell*: Intimate porcine musk and raw timber.
*Habitat*: Most numerous in Appalachia, but with sightings across Nebraska, from Dakota County to Omaha.
*Size*: 585cm
*Contents*: Swine below. Hay up top.

As this statue on the high street attests, A. E. Housman lived for a time in the West Midlands town of Bromsgrove, Worcestershire.

unchangedness and time-defying stillness' as she described it — and track down the man who'd evoked it so vividly from far across the sea.

They couldn't have presented a greater contrast, the young, independent and ambitious American woman at the gate who'd grown up on the prairies of Nebraska and the middle-aged loner English-classics professor inside the house, once described by a fellow don as being 'descended from a long line of maiden aunts'. It was the unlikeliest of settings for the unlikeliest of literary encounters, the vigorously youthful twentieth century crashing into the dusty old nineteenth, the new world barging in on the old.

Willa Cather was steeped in the new world, having been born a seventh-generation Virginian on her grandmother's farm in the Back Creek Valley in 1873. When she was nine the family moved to Nebraska, eventually settling in the small town of Red Cloud where the prairies and vast skies of the frontier made a profound impression on Cather and would fire the narrative of *O Pioneers!*. 'The shaggy grass country had gripped me with a passion I have never been able to shake,' she wrote in 1921. 'It has been the happiness and curse of my life.'

In 1890 she moved to Lincoln, Nebraska, to study science and medicine at the state university, where she also became an arts reviewer and columnist for the *Nebraska State Journal*. That's how she first came across *A Shropshire Lad* in 1897, a discovery that would transform her literary life. It was, she wrote in 1900, a work of such 'exquisite grace of form and delicacy of fancy I scarcely know its equal'.

Accompanied by Isabelle McClung, with whom she had developed an intensely deep friendship that many identify as the love of her life, Cather arrived in Liverpool on the SS *Noordland* from Philadelphia on the rainy morning of 26 June 1902. She found Britain in a curious state of flux: Edward VII's coronation had been set for that day, but his appendicitis caused its postponement and the Boer War had ended less than a month earlier. Cather walked streets festooned with bunting through which subdued Liverpudlians wandered; people who had 'nothing of the smartness and neatness and trimness of an American crowd'.

---

**6. NEBRASKA STATE JOURNAL**

This, the first newspaper serving Nebraska's state capital Lincoln, was founded in 1867 as the *Nebraska Commonwealth*, later becoming the *Nebraska State Journal*, the *Lincoln Journal* and, after merging with the *Lincoln Star* in 1995, the *Lincoln Journal Star*, whose current arts columnist and reviewer L. Kent Wolgamott recommends *Eva Hesse*, Marcie Begleiter's movie about the 1960s postminimalist sculptor, and Drive-By Truckers' latest album, *American Band*.

# O PIONEERS!

The women travelled through Chester, Ludlow and Shrewsbury in search of Housman, with Cather dashing off travel articles for the *Journal* as they went, but while thrilled to recognise much of the landscape from the verses, there was little trace of the poet himself.

'In short I found everything except Housman,' Cather wrote in a later letter. 'Of him not a legend, not a button or feather or mark.'

She arrived in London in mid July, finding 'a wilderness of bigness and strangeness and newness' while staying at a Temperance Hotel on King Street in the east of the city. Having somehow managed to coax Housman's home address from his publisher, Cather, accompanied by McClung and another friend, Dorothy Canfield, a future social reformer who was studying Romance languages in Paris, planned her doorstepping of the poet to whom she was a 'bond slave, mentally'.

An office building now stands on the site of the hotel. It's a quiet, narrow thoroughfare whose shade is welcome on a hot day and where it's possible to imagine three young American women stepping out into the sunshine in their long skirts and ribboned hats, bustling off to catch the bus from the shadow of St Paul's Cathedral and growing apprehensively quieter as their journey wound north towards Highgate. Then the last walk uphill to 17 North Road, a pause at the gate, an exchange of glances and a confident stride to the front door.

Nobody knows for certain what happened next, as no definitive account remains. Cather, fiercely private, destroyed most of her correspondence, but it's clear the experience was a watershed for her. Ford Madox Ford, the pathologically exaggerating English novelist, later published an apocryphal version that cast Cather as the Pooterish representative of a Pittsburgh ladies' *Shropshire Lad* Society pressing on Housman a golden laurel wreath, but the truth seems to revolve more around a sense of disappointment, embarrassment and shattered illusions.

In a letter to a friend the following year, she alluded to 'quite the most horrible boarding house I ever explored'. She lamented Housman's 'gaunt, grey and embittered' countenance and 'the poor man's shoes and cuffs and the state of the carpet in his little hole of a study'. It was a long way from the Housman she'd imagined, the soulful poet who had 'eaten the bitter bread of exile and trod the hostile streets of great cities'.

It seems the encounter was a supremely awkward one for Cather, with Housman caught off-guard by the arrival of his unexpected American visitors. He became briefly animated in conversation with Canfield about her studies, but the stilted pleasantries were clearly far from the homage of which the fledgling novelist had dreamed. When the long silences grew too excruciating the women left, and as Cather reached the end of the path she dissolved into tears.

Cather went on to huge success with novels like *O Pioneers!*, *My Ántonia* and the Pulitzer Prize-winning *One of Ours*, and appeared on the cover of *Time* in 1931. Ill health and family tragedy blighted her later years, but right to the end her thoughts often turned back to that summer afternoon in north London.

Cather had intended to set down 'a careful and considered account of that visit for persons who are interested', but never did. In 1947 she wrote to her old friend Dorothy Canfield, soliciting her memories. Canfield's reply landed on the doormat of the author's Manhattan apartment on 24 April, the day Cather died of a cerebral haemorrhage.

## 7. THE BUS

The address remains highly convenient for bus travel, with the 143 (Archway Station to Brent Cross Shopping Centre), 214 (Finsbury Square to Highgate) and 603 (Swiss Cottage Station to Princes Avenue) all stopping directly outside.

## 8. NORTH ROAD

Housman is not the only literary great associated with this north London thoroughfare. Just opposite 17 North Road is Highgate School, the elite learning institution whose former pupils include Alex Comfort, author of *The Joy of Sex*.

It's an incongruous thought, this most American of authors standing at the gate of a house in a leafy, north London suburb where it's a short distance to the front door, but for her those few yards of paving stones are at once as wide as an ocean, as vast as a prairie and as undulating as the Shropshire hills. Whatever the whole truth of the encounter, Willa Cather was never the same again, throwing off the shackles of her 'bond slavery' and producing some of America's finest fiction.

> CHARLIE CONNELLY is a bestselling author from London. His most pioneering moment occurred in 2010 when he put his cricket bat under his arm and struck out west, arriving at the western tip of Valentia Island off the western edge of County Kerry to play the westernmost cover drive in European history, as noted in the *Wisden Cricketer's Almanack*.

---

MEMORY

AMANDA FORTINI's childhood summers at her father's in Kansas stretched out endlessly — a vast, empty and, it being the 1980s, internet-free expanse. What else was there to do but while away the hours in increasingly inventive ways? Until, one day, she opened the only door she had been told not to.

# DO NOT ENTER

Kansas City, where I spent my adolescent and teenage summers visiting my father, was only 512 miles south-west of suburban Chicago, where I lived full-time with my mother, but to my younger self, it might as well have been a foreign country. For one thing, this part of the Great Plains Midwest was inflected with elements of the South — the region was bitterly divided during the Civil War, and Missouri had been a slave-holding state. (My father, a lawyer for a telecommunications company, lived on the Kansas side of Kansas City, but he worked downtown, in Kansas City, Missouri, and we spent plenty of time there.) The South was present in the twang of the neighbour kids' accents, in the barbecue I was suposed to love but didn't unless the sauce was sugary and bland, in the antiquated attitudes you'd encounter if you went too far out of the city. I didn't know what any of this meant, really. I just knew Kansas felt different somehow.

It was also hotter in Kansas, and more humid. Your clothes were always slightly, grossly, damp, like you'd pulled them too soon from the dryer. At night, my younger sister and I, who were forced to share a room — we were thirteen months apart, and everyone glommed us together — would strip down to our underpants and lie on our bed's fitted sheet, nothing else beneath us, not even pillows. Many times we'd sleep with our heads at the foot of the bed because that's where the fan was, that heavy-breather exhaling its lungful of hot air. We knew that it was sweltering in that house because my dad was too cheap to turn on the air conditioner — our towels all said Marriot, and we ate with paper napkins swiped from McDonald's — but we didn't dare mention this to him. We just whined to each other that the nights were sweatier and more sleepless than any back home.

But my main issue with Kansas City was that I had no friends there. I hung around with my siblings — my other sister was five years younger than me; my stepbrother was four years younger — as well as the two freckled little boys who lived across the street. But I didn't know anyone my own age, and there seemed to be no prospect of meeting someone. We lived in a residential subdivision in a suburb bordered by roads busy with cars swooshing past; there wasn't any place I could walk to. I felt trapped, stranded in the middle of nowhere. Or in Kansas, which, as Dorothy knew, can feel like the same thing.

Those summers were relentlessly boring, as suffocating and unyielding as the heat. I was a sensitive kid, prone to allergies and hurt feelings, but also obstinate and mentally tough, and I treated the days that yawned before me as a personal challenge. I'm not retrospectively embroidering when I say that I honestly thought of myself as a kind of pioneer out on the plains, tasked with my own survival, which meant keeping my days full and my spirits up. I knew what pioneers were, and I romanticised and idolised them. I'd read all the *Little House on the Prairie* books, and I religiously watched the show based on the series. As young girls, my sister and I even invented a game we called 'Pioneer'. This consisted of pretending to grow and cook food, constructing lean-tos with blanket and pillows — otherwise known as forts — and making a faux trek west, where we panned for gold using pie tins.

There was at least one way in which being 'heavy bored' — to borrow a phrase from John Berryman — at my dad's house wasn't so bad. He had a full cable package in an era when most people in our milieu did not; that meant MTV and HBO. We weren't supposed to lie around watching TV all day, and certain shows we were forbidden to watch entirely. When the HBO guide arrived, my stepmother would flip through it, circling her recommendations and crossing out everything verboten. She left us with options like *The Bad News Bears*, the baseball movie about a team of lovable losers in which Tatum O'Neal plays a tomboy who helps them get to the championship; and *Fraggle Rock*, the sprightly Jim Henson show about various cave-dwelling creatures (the Fraggles vaguely resembled colourful troll dolls) that learn thinly veiled progressive lessons.

We ignored her, and watched what we wanted to watch. Our babysitter, who was barely older than I was, didn't care what we did, as long as we left her alone. We became obsessive devotees of, among other illicit entertainments, like Nintendo and Bangles videos, a movie called *Eddie and the Cruisers* — the story of a rock star's mysterious disappearance told in flashbacks, *Citizen Kane*-style. Some days, I never changed out of my pyjamas. At 5pm, when I heard the garage door rumble and my stepmother's car pull in (minutes later she'd enter, dressed in a pencil skirt and commuter Reeboks), I scrambled upstairs to throw on clothes.

We were supposed to be spending our summer engaged in wholesome activities, like going to the public pool. My father and

Still from 'The Last Farewell', 1984's explosive final episode of *Little House on the Prairie*.

stepmother insisted we pass the day there, presumably splashing cheerfully around with friends we didn't have. But have you ever spent eight hours outside in sun-reflecting water on a 100-degree day? I got sunburns that will surely come back to haunt me. I also hated going to the pool because I was flat-chested and skinny as an asparagus stalk, not to mention polka-dotted with mosquito bites. In my opinion, a swimsuit threw all of this into grotesque relief. Luckily, our babysitter didn't like going either; there were boys she wanted to avoid. We lied and said we'd gone, opting, instead, to remain parked in front of the television.

The minutes dripped past — one, then another, and another — droplets from a leaking faucet. Do you remember how long days were in the years before cell phones and the internet? How did we fill all those hours kids now spend texting, talking, posting, liking, infiltrating each other's boredom, stealing each other's solitude? I scratched my mosquito bites, using my fingernails to brand them with Xs. I jogged. I handwrote letters not only to my boyfriend back home, but also to every one of my friends, my grandparents, and random people I'd met at camps, detailing for them the infinitesimal fluctuations of my days. Often, I read late into the night, keeping a list of books as I completed them. *The Outsiders. The Pigman. Dracula. Frankenstein.* Once a week my dad would take my siblings and me to the library, where he'd allow us to check out a handful of books. I'd attempt to ration mine for the week. But I'd always deplete my stash days before our next trip, so I'd furtively read whatever I found around the house, like V.C. Andrews' *Flowers in the Attic* series, about a pair of incestuous siblings locked in an attic by their horrid old grandmother. I knew that, should I get caught, these books would be treated as more taboo than the shows on HBO.

Eventually, our collective boredom led us downstairs, to the cavernous unfinished basement. Its cold, smooth concrete floors and total lack of furniture gave rise to a game we called 'Zoo'. We'd set up our stuffed animals around the room, then push each other up and down the length of it in an old TV cart — this was the 'zoo trolley' — to view them. If anything signals how under-stimulated we were, it's this game. But the real lure of the basement was my dad's 'workroom', which was adjacent to the main room. We were told never to go in there.

We did, of course. We cracked the door open a few times before we worked up the courage to enter. From the threshold, we saw towers of boxes; it all seemed tame enough. Inside, though, my sister and I found what appeared to be everything my dad had ever bought, everything he'd ever used, everything he'd ever owned — hell, everything he'd ever encountered — boxed and labelled in neat all-capitals hand-writing. There were boxes that read OLD TOOTHBRUSHES and boxes that read BASEBALL CAPS. T-SHIRTS. OLD CLOTHES. KIDS' ART PROJECTS. I pulled back the top on that last one to find clay medallions and yarn god's eyes (those creations that come from weaving yarn around two sticks) I'd made in preschool, a decade earlier.

As soon as my sister and I saw all of this, we knew we shouldn't be there. It was a version of the primal scene, like walking in on a parent having sex, but kind of worse. We didn't yet know about 'hoarding' or 'OCD', but we knew it was unusual behaviour, and that our father had wanted to keep it hidden. Even at eleven years old, I understood that this was a fateful moment, one I would not easily forget. It would gnaw at me. I went back a few more times, alone and in secret. I spent so little time with my father apart from these summers; this was like roaming through the precincts of his brain.

The room and its tidily hoarded contents seemed to contain the key to something important — to my father, my history, possibly to my own self — some notion that was just beyond my ability to grasp. My mind still returns to that memory, that room, like a tongue pokes around at a sore tooth. Boredom and isolation are uncomfortable, even upsetting but they can also lead us to places we might not explore otherwise, including those dark places where the truth is kept.

AMANDA FORTINI has written for *The New York Times*, *The New Yorker*, and the *Los Angeles Review of Books*, among other publications. She is a contributing editor at *Elle Magazine*. Although she spent more than a decade in New York City and LA, she now lives in Livingston, Montana, a town of 7,000 on the westernmost edge of the Great Plains.

**FLYOVER**
Corrugated grasslands surround a lake in the Great Plains, that rather vast prairie-like part of the earth's surface that spans from Canada all the way to the border between the US and Mexico.

# Here it is. The new Penguin Donkey, exclusively for Happy Readers.

This obliging creature holds up to ninety Pocket Penguin paperbacks in its two panniers, carries a number of issues of The Happy Reader in the middle and provides a convenient chair-side table for your tray of hors d'oeuvres, coffee cups, glass, ashtray, knitting or anything else you want to keep beside you. A limited edition of the celebrated Isokon Penguin Donkey Mark II, originally designed by the late Ernest Race, is a talking-point centrepiece for any room.

The Donkey is available in a number of colours, corresponding to the different colours of the Pocket Penguins series. The finish is unaffected by hot cups or spilt drinks; a surface that wipes clean with a touch. The horizontal shelves are horizontal because Penguins *should* lie flat. They keep better that way and you can read every title from your chair. The upright spaces? They take maps, hardbacks and whatever else might fit.

This limited-edition version of the Isokon Penguin Donkey II is being produced in colour batches of only five, so no more than four fellow readers around the world will have the same Donkey as you.

**Find out more at thehappyreader.com/isokon**

# LETTERS

The interesting vocabulary of high society, and a valiant adventure in Clarissa Dalloway's footsteps.

Dear Happy Reader,

I much enjoyed reading all about the plummy parties in the last issue of *THR*.

I am now obsessed with the 'Bystander' section of the *Tatler* website, which is full of 21st birthdays, polo tournaments, galas hosted by the most proper names in Surrey, Mayfair and Ayrshire. The party descriptions are great; littered with phrases such as 'Barbour-clad', 'golly' and 'mini burgers'.

All the best,
Georgia Haire, London, UK

---

Dear Seb,

My recent trip to London saw me walking various streets with my copy of *THR7* open on the page of the Dalloway Puzzle. I'm not usually one for crosswords, but I felt compelled to give it a go. My mum and I dedicated the Friday we arrived to attempting it, and we stuck to our plan. After guessing that 1A is BEN (?) we began our adventures with 1D. We found what appeared to be (at the time) Bloomsbury Square and sat in it, looking for a Statesman and a pillar-box. There was only one statue, so we walked towards it, pencil at the ready.

'If his name doesn't begin with B...' I said, walking up to it, only to find that his name was Francis Duke of Bedford. 'Bed? Could it be Bed?' There was even a pillar-box across the road. Looking back, we might have cut it a bit short and were wandering through Russell Square clutching at straws.

However, all was not lost, as I believe 7D is PELICAN and 16D is NELSON. I thought finding the 'Figure between Peel and Disraeli' would be easy, and I found Peel, but couldn't find Disraeli to save my life. They must have moved him that day; it's the only logical solution.

Speaking of solutions... may I have them?
Yours, eternally puzzled,
Jade Moore
Beeston, Nottingham, UK

*The Happy Reader replies: Yes, you may! The solution is at the bottom of this page.*

---

Dear Editor,

I was innocently reading Will Self's thoughts 'ON BIG BEN' (*THR7*) when Bongggg!, he wrote: 'every infant Londoner was also aware that the zero degree of latitude passed through our city'. Hold it, I thought - that's the Equator, isn't it? So then I had to revert to my own schoolgirl trick. The long longitude lines (like the Greenwich meridian) run north and south between the Poles. The lines of latitude run laterally or sideways. Because you see, Will, I could never keep them straight either.

Best regards,
Carrie Drummond
Cromer, Norfolk UK

Send your thoughts on the magazine and/or Books of the Season to letters@thehappyreader.com or The Happy Reader, Penguin Books, 80 Strand, London WC2R 0RL. If yours makes the issue, as well as the pleasure of seeing your name in print, you'll receive a free copy of the next Book of the Season.

DALLOWAY PUZZLE SOLUTION

Across: 1. Fac 3. Tea 4. Jehangir 6. Poppadom 9. LL 11. BIS 13. Regina 14. Arabia 15. RVP 17. Grenville 19. 20. Aveenue 22. Art. Down: 1. Fox 2. Gandhi 3. TR 5. William Pitt 7. Pelican 8. Coach 10. Peter 11. Bar 12. Sap 16. Valour 17. Gold 18. SA 21. EJ

# THE HAPPY READER

The Happy Reader is Penguin's magazine-based book club, enjoyed by avid readers all over the world. Subscribe by visiting thehappyreader.com.

# THE NEXT BOOK

Every issue of *The Happy Reader* is in the orbit of a single work of literature, a classic. Or, to borrow Italo Calvino's definition, 'a book that has never finished saying what it has to say.' Classics come in many forms, so the magazine has delved into everything from Gothic fiction to travel writing, from Japanese philosophy to apocalyptic sci-fi. Next we'll be turning our telescope towards *Treasure Island*, Robert Louis Stevenson's timeless yet strangely underrated adventure novel.

Following this current issue, *The Happy Reader* will be published twice a year, in summer and winter, meaning *Treasure Island*, that dazzling yarn of pirates, treasure and bloodthirsty betrayal will be Book of the Season for the coming summer. Everyone knows the names Jim Hawkins and Long John Silver, and everyone, upon hearing the words 'treasure' and 'island' in close succession, immediately thinks of tropical seas, secret maps and curved swords. Yet many have come by these associations without ever actually reading the book. It's easy to overlook the fact that, as well as a gripping story, *Treasure Island* is a work of spectacular literary genius.

The next issue of *The Happy Reader* is due for publication in June 2017. Readers are advised to pick up a copy of Robert Louis Stevenson's masterpiece before then, and are encouraged to get in touch with any insights, ideas or anecdotes in the meantime by writing to us at letters@thehappyreader.com.

Jacket for *Treasure Island*, originally published in 1883.